BIG
DEAL

BIG
DEAL

A MEMOIR FROM THE
WONDERFUL WORLD OF BRIDGE

AUGIE BOEHM

BRIDGE WORLD BOOKS • NEW YORK

ISBN: 978-0-9753419-7-1
This book includes previously published material, used by permission of
the American Contract Bridge League and Bridge World Magazine Inc.
Cover design by Geneviève Leloup
Back-cover photograph by Bachrach

www.bridgeworld.com

Bridge World Books • New York

PREFACE

In a sense, everyone who influenced my bridge development played a role in producing this book. The most influential you will meet by name in the upcoming pages.

To single out a few, there are my editors, Brent Manley of the American Contract Bridge League's *Bridge Bulletin*, and, especially, Jeff Rubens of *The Bridge World*. Their guidance and wise counsel over the years provided encouragement and honed my writing skills.

Closer to the bone are the Boehms, George and Alice, my parents who respectively taught and nurtured my bridge. And most important is Melissa Hubner, my wife, the most dedicated rooter, supporter, and invaluable advisor. On my personal rating system, she is off the scales.

Augie Boehm
October 2013

TABLE OF CONTENTS

INTRODUCTION

Bridge is the world's greatest game. It rivals chess in analytical complexity and adds the crucial elements of partnership collaboration and psychology. There's enough luck to pique the interest of the average player, and enough skill to reward the expert. Bridge can be played at virtually any age—children will find it a superb building block for concentration, logic and socialization. Seniors enjoy the companionship, and there is medical evidence that regular doses of bridge seem to diminish the chance of dementia. The game is enjoyable at all levels, from coffee klatch to cutthroat. It can engage the keenest minds for a lifetime, and it is the most democratic of sports because a novice may enter an event and compete against the best in the world.

Perhaps you know all this. Possibly, you played bridge when you were young, then put it aside while you raised a family or pursued a career. Like many baby boomers, you returned to bridge later in life and found it changed.

While you were away, it really changed—alerts, silent bidding, lots and lots of conventions, and more. How did it get to be this way? This book will help explain. If you are a relative newcomer, it might interest you to know the background of the world's greatest card game. If you are a tournament veteran, enjoy some nostalgic reminiscences.

I have spent countless hours reading, writing, teaching, playing, directing, being involved with the Laws, or simply thinking about bridge. I started very young and was fortunate to enjoy personal contact with many of the bridge legends who helped make this game great. In addition, I've had an inside track to every avenue available to a bridge professional. During the significant changes over the past half-century, I've been either a witness or a participant. In effect, my memoir encapsulates much of modern bridge history.

Sit over my shoulder and kibitz competitions ranging from the highest-level tournaments to "The Bucket of Blood." Take note of how the conduct and ethics of players have shifted dramatically. How did the enormous proliferation of conventions and systems take hold? What was the impact of the great cheating scandals?

My teaching experience has taken me from the carriage trade to cruise ships to a penitentiary. In this book, you'll find glimpses of Omar Sharif, Stephen Sondheim, the Rockefellers, bridge legends, and people high and low who populate the wonderful world of bridge. This is a group of highly intelligent, sometimes peculiar, often funny people. Be prepared to laugh.

I am also a trained musician. I have thirty-five Carnegie-Weill classical solo piano recitals behind me, and counting. This book includes chapters in which bridge and music overlap; that has been part of the fun, and there are some interesting intersections.

Many of the bridge legends in these pages are dead, but unquestionably their acute observations and timeless insights should endure and endear, another purpose behind this book, which can be read by non-players and beginners for the stories and the personalities. However, even a moderately-experienced player will profit all the more from the deals and analyses. And if bridge is exciting or makes you chuckle, please pass the news along to the next generation.

CHAPTER 1

IN THE BEGINNING

Before I was ten, I was playing tournament bridge. A bridge-playing friend recently asked me what that world of the 1950's was like. She marveled that there were enough youngsters to justify a tournament event; she believed that even in New York City, where I was raised, it couldn't have been easy to gather a dozen or more kids to compete in a duplicate, perhaps shortened to accommodate restless young people. When I started, there weren't a dozen kids or even a table of four—I was the only one. Club duplicates were populated entirely by adults, the game ran the full-length three hours, there were no masterpoint restrictions, and so novices and Life Masters competed together. There were a smaller number of Life Masters then, and the title meant far more. Nowadays, with an entirely different tournament structure, masterpoints are much easier to win, because players never need to play above their masterpoint classification. A player can become a Life Master without ever playing against one, and there are now so many Life Masters that subdivisions have been created—Silver Life Master, Gold Life Master, etc.

In club duplicates back then, a newcomer slugged it out with vastly more experienced players, in hopes of eventually earning a small fraction of one masterpoint, written on a pink slip. You tucked those slips away in a safe place, and when you accumulated one full point, you mailed them to The American Contract Bridge League (ACBL) to be recorded. Progress along the masterpoint trail was slow, but progress along the learning curve was quicker. Competing against players with greater skills, you took your lumps, but you noticed what the strong players and experts did, and soon you were avoiding basic errors and advancing through the ranks. Of course, there is always a new error to make, even for top experts, but that is part of bridge's lifetime charm.

At my earliest duplicates, one accommodation was made for me—since I was small for my age, I was permitted to sit on a telephone book to see over the top of the table. My partners were Mike Grenthal, a seventeen-year-old neighbor who became a lifetime friend, and my father, George, a science writer and noted bridge expert who taught me the game. Tournament players who are familiar with the lebensohl convention, standard fare for serious pairs, may know that the convention was first described by my father, George, in *The Bridge World* magazine in November and December 1970. (My father spelled the name with an initial lower-case letter, because the person he mistakenly had thought invented it, Ken Lebensold, disowned it. That spelling has stuck.)

My father taught me and my mother, Alice, at the same time. As an exercise, we were given legal yellow sheets filled with card combinations to play, such as ace-jack-seven-six-deuce in dummy facing queen-nine-eight-five-four in your hand. To maximize the chance for five tricks, the first decision is to finesse instead of playing the ace; hoping to drop a singleton king is against the odds. That's probabilities, but there's more.

Best is to lead the queen and plan to finesse if second-hand plays low. The queen is a stronger play than leading low to dummy's jack, because it picks up the whole suit when second-hand is dealt all three missing cards. Low to the jack eventually loses a trick to the king-ten, but starting with the queen allows a later proven finesse of dummy's nine if second hand covers.

Conventions, the sexy part of the game, are what the tournament players yearn to learn, but card combinations, often neglected, are the nuts and bolts. It's impossible to become a first-rate declarer or defender without understanding the underlying principles that govern card play. The ACBL's current *Official Encyclopedia of Bridge* devotes 50 single-spaced oversize pages to card combinations. It's doubtful that anyone knows every suit combination, but no winning player can afford to ignore them. Detailed thinking is important for success at bridge, and I was shown the way at a formative age.

Occasionally, I was permitted to extend my bedtime by half an hour to kibitz one of my father's home games. One evening, I watched Abe Schwartz open the bidding one heart without a heart in his hand and about 3 high-card points. I had been instructed that a kibitzer says nothing and acts neutral, but I could hardly stand it.

When the players took a brief break for coffee, I followed my father to the kitchen, where he was brewing a Chemex.

"How can you play with such a partner," I sputtered, "and for money, too. Mr. Schwartz doesn't know the first thing about the game."

My father chuckled, and that's when I learned what a psych was (a deliberate bluff). Psychic bidding is rare these days, even frowned upon, but it was commonplace in the earliest, halcyon days of contract bridge.

*   *   *

Harold S. Vanderbilt, America's Cup yachtsman and heir to the Vanderbilt fortune, is credited with developing the modern game of bridge. In the autumn of 1925, while on his yacht with three bridge-playing friends, they found themselves waiting to pass through the Panama Canal. Confined to ship because of a local quarantine, Vanderbilt decided to test some ideas he had been mulling to improve auction bridge, the current form of the game. The players liked Vanderbilt's idea that you were required to bid to game or slam to earn the scoring bonus—in auction bridge, if declarer made ten tricks in spades, he received the game bonus even if he had bid only two. When the ship returned to New York, the new game, contract bridge, spread rapidly, in large part because of Vanderbilt's social standing and enthusiasm, but also because it was a clear improvement—high rewards only came with increased risk. By 1929, contract bridge had largely replaced auction bridge and whist, early forerunners of bridge with British roots. The Great Depression ruined many lives, but it was a boost for bridge. In the early 1930's, when many families had less disposable income, inviting friends over for supper and bridge became a popular, inexpensive entertainment. Ely Culbertson, a Romanian émigré, was the first expert to become rich from promoting himself and the new game. In 1931, his *Blue Book* outsold all others—not just bridge books, *all* books. Today, with so many avenues open for entertainment or distraction, it is impossible to imagine what a central role bridge played in Depression-ridden America.

Culbertson developed his own system, which featured a one-over-one forcing response (e.g.: one diamond — pass — one spade could not be passed), a revolutionary idea for its day. The British system of bidding demanded that a player jump when holding extra strength—the more you have, the more you bid—which seemed intuitively sensible. Culbertson was one of the first to recognize that the opposite is actually true—the more you have, the lower and slower you should bid, as long as those bids are forcing, requiring partner to take another bid. In this manner, a pair can thoroughly investigate its combined potential. Jumps are best reserved for impeding the opponents, to prevent them from exploring their own possibilities. Bridge, like all great games, is a study in developing your own position while blocking the opposition.

The Depression era was prime time for bridge. Culbertson made movie shorts in Hollywood, and he staged some well-publicized challenge matches against British and American teams. These matches were covered in the daily newspapers and even live, on radio. The participants dressed in formal wear, and the matches were often front-page news.

The Culbertson-Lenz match, which took place between December 1931 and January 1932, was billed as "The Bridge Battle of the Century." Bridge was making its first great impact in the United States, and Ely and Josephine Culbertson portrayed themselves as a young married couple, opposed by the reactionary forces of auction bridge, contract's predecessor. The match captured the general public's attention, as well as being a constant topic at the bridge table. At the end of this book, this famous match will resurface.

Bridge also made news in another way—the celebrated Bennett murder case. In 1929, Myrtle Bennett shot and killed her husband, John, after a most cantankerous evening of bridge at their home. In the early editions of the *Official Encyclopedia of Bridge*, a deal was given that provoked the fatal event where John both misbid and misplayed a four-spade contract. Myrtle had endured enough; she went to their bedroom for a revolver, and shot her husband dead in front of their horrified guests.

BENNETT MURDER

This historic tragedy took place in Kansas City, MO, on September 29, 1929. The victim was 36-year-old John G. Bennett, a prosperous perfume salesman, who met his death as a result of a game of contract in which he played with his wife, Myrtle, against another married couple, Charles and Mayme Hofman. Mrs. Bennett became so infuriated at her husband's play that she shot him following a bitter quarrel. She was tried for murder in March of 1931 and was acquitted. The alleged deal was this:

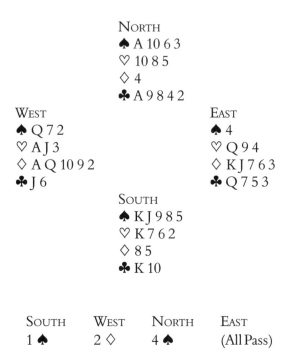

NORTH
♠ A 10 6 3
♡ 10 8 5
◇ 4
♣ A 9 8 4 2

WEST
♠ Q 7 2
♡ A J 3
◇ A Q 10 9 2
♣ J 6

EAST
♠ 4
♡ Q 9 4
◇ K J 7 6 3
♣ Q 7 5 3

SOUTH
♠ K J 9 8 5
♡ K 7 6 2
◇ 8 5
♣ K 10

SOUTH	WEST	NORTH	EAST
1 ♠	2 ◇	4 ♠	(All Pass)

Bennett opened the bidding without sufficient values for an opening bid and suffered an unusually heavy penalty. However, four spades was not an impossible contract, given the actual distribution. West opened the diamond ace and shifted to the club jack. Bennett actually won this with the king and set about drawing trumps, ending his chances. Instead he should have ruffed a diamond, led a trump to his king and continued with his last club. When West followed, he should have gone up with the ace and led the club nine, intending to discard a heart if it was not covered. If East covered with the queen, Bennett should ruff and let West overruff. If at this point West should lead either red suit, Bennett would have had his 10 tricks. Only a trump lead at this point could keep South from making his contract—and saving his life.

The episode was entertainingly described at length by Alexander Woollcott in an essay from *While Rome Burns* (1934).

*   *   *

Those acquainted with the Bennett murder case had their beliefs upended in 2009, when *The Devil's Tickets* by Gary Pomerantz exploded the long-standing myth about the fateful deal. There was no fateful deal, or at least none that any of the participants could remember. The visiting couple, Mr. and Mrs. Hofman, were too distressed to remember any details, and Myrtle Bennett was prostrate with remorse. None of the players was above average ability, and most average players have great trouble remembering details of deals they have played, even in non-traumatic circumstances.

Ely Culbertson hired Sidney Lenz, another prominent bridge authority, to investigate the dramatic incident that had captured the public's attention. Lenz created the four-spade deal out of thin air—and bridge anthologies ran it for the next 75 years as gospel truth. You mustn't believe everything you read.

When Myrtle Bennett was acquitted, some called it temporary insanity; some wags even thought the judge must have been a bridge player, and they condemned John's bidding and play. In fact, the jury found the prosecution's case unproven and that the shooting might have been accidental. However, on the day the verdict was announced, the country club in Kansas City, Missouri announced that husbands and wives would no longer be permitted to play as partners in their upcoming tournaments. Myrtle Bennett lived a long and rather prosperous life, but it is said that she had trouble finding bridge partners.

CHAPTER 2

MY EARLY YEARS

My bridge development was hugely accelerated by the expert company my father kept. By the time I was twelve, I had had the rare privilege of playing one duplicate session each with Edgar Kaplan, Alfred Sheinwold, and Tobias Stone, legends of the game. All were gentle and generous with their advice, even Stoney, who was known for his volatile temper and sarcastic wit. Years later, when I was an adult and better able to withstand abuse, he unleashed his stinging barbs when we played. Years after that, we became friends—he attended the wedding party after my first marriage. When I was a lad, he was as soft and encouraging as could be. He autographed a copy of the Roth-Stone book, *Bridge is a Partnership Game*, inscribing, "If The System makes you a better player than Dad, just blame me." That book was part of my required summer reading, along with the more conventional books that schools assigned youngsters. My schooling was actually quite normal. I played and enjoyed sports, and I diligently practiced the piano at an early age under the tutelage of my grandmother, Minnie. The unusual aspect of my upbringing was that I often kept company with adults. Peer relationships with girls or boys my own age suffered, and it took a long time to catch up and feel comfortable. However, this evolution was perhaps inevitable—when I attended my first dance in sixth grade, I tried to interest my date in negative doubles and Beethoven sonatas. When that failed, the dynastic New York Yankees. For her, one date was enough.

Mike Grenthal, my older friend and neighbor, was now attending the University of Virginia. In the summer of 1960, we played in a sectional tournament in Brooklyn that was a regular part of the New York bridge calendar. In those days, there was something of an inter-borough rivalry between Brooklyn and the rest of New York, probably attached to the old Dodger-Yankee rivalry. In bridge, as in baseball, Brooklyn was usually on the short end. *The New York Times* columnist, Albert Morehead, took notice in his column dated August 1, 1960.

He reported that a thirteen-year old lad, one August Boehm, "stole the show" by finishing high up in the overalls of the men's pairs. In a flight of fancy, he added that my partner, Michael J. Grenthal, 21 years old, was my pupil and that I had taught him how to play bridge.

Of course, I was elated at a *New York Times* mention, but Mike considered a lawsuit to force the newspaper to print a retraction about his being my student; at college, he took a lot of ribbing from his fraternity. The student-teacher part was Morehead's fiction, but, in fact, I already had some teaching experience, although not at bridge. At the private school I attended, by the fourth grade I happened to be the second-best chess player. Richard Neff, somewhat older, was the best, and, as an adult, he became a serious bridge player. Games expertise tends to cross-pollinate. The mother of one of my classmates hired me to improve her son's chess game—I saved that five-dollar bill as a souvenir for years. I recall playing a game against my classmate's father, at best an average player, thinking that an over-my-shoulder approach would be a good way to instruct my classmate. As I played Dad and mowed him down, I offered copious commentary on why his moves were weak and mine were strong. It's a small miracle I wasn't murdered.

The summer after my session with Grenthal, my bridge career took a leap. The first-ever national championship for Junior players (maximum age 19) was to be staged in Washington, D.C. in conjunction with the Summer Nationals (now the NABC).

B. Jay Becker, one of the bridge immortals, had a son, Mike, who was 17 and already an accomplished player. B. Jay contacted my father and suggested that the two boys form a partnership with an eye to competing in Washington. I was all for it, and Mike and I played a practice duplicate in the New York area. How to form a "serious" partnership, or at least a partnership preparing for a serious event, was a new step for me, and my father, ever supportive, found ways to assist. The following is reprinted from *The Bridge World*, March, 1962. Remember, George Boehm was a writer first, a bridge expert second.

Let's Keep the Bidding Simple
by George A.W. Boehm

Last summer my son August, aged fourteen at the time, was headed for Washington to play in the National Teen-Year Pairs event with B. Jay Becker's younger son, Mike. The boys had had only one practice session, but Mike assured Augie they could straighten out their partnership understandings during the four-hour train ride from New York.

"What are you two going to play?" I asked Augie the evening before his departure.

"Nothing much," he replied with the disdainful sniff of a confirmed Roth-Stoner. "Just go-as-you-please, with Stayman, weak jump-overcalls, and maybe weak two-bids."

That set me to thinking. Just how many understandings ought to be established by a partnership that is ostensibly playing Standard American? So, I sat down at the typewriter and dashed off a list of points the boys really should discuss. The number of items stunned me, yet I suspected that in haste or ignorance I had omitted some obvious ones.

Opening Suit Bids: When, if ever, can a four-card major be opened? How light are minimum openings in each position? Ever psych?

Opening Notrumps: What range? Ever shaded in third or fourth position? Can they include a worthless doubleton? Under what circumstances can opener rebid or double freely?

Responses to Suit Bids: Does one notrump deny three cards in support of partner's major? What does a free raise promise? Does a one-notrump response to a minor absolutely deny a four-card major? Is a single raise of a major mildly constructive? How do you handle a hand that is a little too good for a single raise? Is this sequence forcing for one round or to game?

South	North
1 ♠	2 ♣
2 ♦	2 ♠

With two four-card suits does responder always bid the cheaper? Does a two-over-one guarantee that responder will bid again? Does a two-heart response to one spade promise five hearts? Do you respond one notrump or two diamonds when partner opens one spade and you hold:

$$♠ x x \ ♡ x x x \ ♦ A Q J x x x \ ♣ Q x$$

Responses to Notrump: Forcing or non-forcing Stayman? Can opener rebid two notrump? How does he answer to Stayman with two four-card majors? How does he show a five-card major? Is a three-club or three-diamond response weak? If opponents intervene, what responses are weak, encouraging, forcing?

Rebids: Does opener show extra values by a change of suit at the two-level, e.g.:

South	North
1 ♠	2 ♣
2 ♦	

Does opener promise extra values in these auctions:

South	North
1 ♠	2 ◇
2 NT	

Or:

South	North
1 ♠	2 ◇
3 ◇	

Does he guarantee six spades by either of these two auctions:

South	North
1 ♠	1 NT
2 ♠	

Or:

South	North
1 ♠	2 ♣
2 ♠	

Is a new suit by responder always a one-round force? Are all jumps by responder forcing to game? When can opener's jump rebid or reverse be passed?

Slam Conventions: When is four notrump a natural bid? When is four clubs Gerber? If four clubs asks for aces, how do you ask for kings? How do you respond to Blackwood or Gerber if the opponents intervene? Do you use the grand slam force?

Takeout Doubles: Do they guarantee good distribution, or can doubler be short in an unbid major? Is a jump response to a take-out double forcing for one round? Is a cue-bid forcing to game? When partner's opening bid has been doubled, is your takeout forcing, non-committal, or very weak? Does a redouble promise support for partner's suit? At what level are doubles of opening preempts chiefly for business?

Overcalls: If you respond to partner's overcall with a new suit, is he forced or encouraged to bid again? How about jump take-outs of partner's overcall: forcing, encouraging, or preemptive? How strong are single and double raises of partner's overcall?

Weak Jump-Overcalls: Do they strictly deny any outside defensive values? Are you likely to "operate" with favorable vulnerability and a passing partner? What is the meaning of a jump-overcall when vulnerability is unfavorable?

Miscellaneous Sequences: When is a notrump bid "unusual?" When does it ask for minors and when for unbid suits? When the bidding has gone one heart by West, pass, pass, what strength and distribution does South promise by balancing with an overcall, a jump-overcall, one notrump, two notrump, or a cue-bid? How does vulnerability affect your answers? At high levels, when the bidding has been competitive, do you double to show defensive trump strength or merely to show that you have bid the limit of your hand? Are your doubles in the following three auctions competitive or strictly for business?

SOUTH	WEST	NORTH	EAST
1 ♡	Pass	1 NT	Pass
Pass	Double		

Or:

SOUTH	WEST	NORTH	EAST
1 ♡	Pass	1 ♠	Pass
2 ♡	Double		

Or:

SOUTH	WEST	NORTH	EAST
1 ♡	Pass	1 NT	Pass
2 ♡	Double		

Any reader of *The Bridge World* could doubtless think of dozens of other understandings that are worth discussing with a new partner. The number might be multiplied several fold if you wanted to use such elaborate conventions as negative doubles, inverted minor suit raises, and short-suit tries for game, or if you went into the subtleties of defensive signaling. But even in its simplest form, Standard American bidding calls for a bewildering number of special interpretations. This helps to explain why duplicate played with a steady partner is so different from rubber bridge played in the rough-and-tumble arena of a bridge club.

As the boys left for Washington, I had a sneaking suspicion that I might not have done them a favor. But they won the event—perhaps despite my well-intentioned efforts to solidify their partnership.

[*Editor's note:* George Boehm, an editor of *Fortune* magazine, is one of New York's most versatile bridge experts, able and willing to play any of the principal American bidding systems. However, he leans toward Roth-Stone, a fact that makes us suspect that he is trying to prove that the so-called scientific systems are not the only ones riddled with complexities. (Indeed, this suspicion was confirmed by a phone call to Mr. Boehm.)

His points are well taken, of course, but we can't see that he is making a good case for the scientific systems by saying, "You too!" The thousand-and-one variations of American Standard are deplorable, but the cure scarcely lies in substituting two thousand different understandings.]

*

[*Author's note:* This article was included in the eightieth anniversary awards issue of *The Bridge World*, October 2009, which paid "homage to the spectacular variety of bridge and its literature."]

The Teen-Year pairs attracted general interest. *Sports Illustrated* magazine ran a regular bridge column authored by Charles Goren, for decades the dean of American bridge and a household name. Groucho Marx had Goren as a guest on his quiz show, *You Bet Your Life*, and Goren hosted a nationally-televised Sunday-afternoon program featuring bridge competitions (more on that in a later chapter). Anyway, *Sports Illustrated* sent a photographer to cover our event. When Mike and I arrived, we were seated North-South, a stationary position, so the lighting need not be moved, and at table one, suggesting that we might be the pre-tournament favorite.

I think the staging under the bright lights, with the photographer up on a platform clicking away, must have unnerved our college-age opponents more than us. We both played well and won by a large margin, getting our pictures in the ACBL magazine and a nice mention. Alas, the story never was published in *Sports Illustrated*, I forget why, but it was a most satisfying win, and Mike Becker, in his Hall-of-Fame address, mentioned the event as his first big victory. The next entry is reprinted from the First Edition of the ACBL's *Official Encyclopedia of Bridge*.

CHILDREN

Youth is no bar to contract bridge, and many children play as well as their parents. Among the outstandingly successful children are Mark Goldstein, Hopkins, Minn., who played creditably at the Charity Game of the Summer Nationals in 1962 at the age of seven, appearing later on a panel show in company with the nation's bridge greats; Dianne Barton, San Francisco, who had won over 10 masterpoints at the age of eleven; and August Boehm, New York, who was the youngest player competing in the first National Teen-Year Pairs, winning the title at age thirteen.

*

[*Author's note:* I was actually fourteen, but I was still the youngest competitor. Imagine what this hype could have meant to me and my family then if bridge had translated into today's full football/basketball scholarship, and at current prices.]

*   *   *

Bridge in the 1960's still occupied a significant place in American social life. Photos of that era show women in dresses and men in coat-and-tie. Dwight Eisenhower, recently retired from office, was photographed attending the Washington tournament. He made the cover of the ACBL *Bridge Bulletin* in September, 1961, and inside the magazine he is shown kibitzing Alvin Landy. (Mike Becker and I are photographed after winning the Teen-Year Pairs.)

Charles Goren, Mr. Bridge to a whole generation of players, was active until the mid-1960's, frequently a winner in top-level competition, and America's bridge authority with many best-selling books. Originally a Philadelphia lawyer, he replaced Culbertson as the game's guru and became wealthy and famous. He wasn't the strongest expert of his era, but he surrounded himself with top players.

His regular partner was Helen Sobel, a former showgirl. I met her once at a tournament when she kindly autographed one of her books. She was part of a tiny handful of women players who were accepted as the equal of the best men, and she knew her worth. So did Goren, who gifted her with mink coats and the like. She and Goren always attracted a horde of kibitzers, and during a lull in the action, a sweet older lady drew up her courage to ask Mrs. Sobel, "What is it like, playing with the world's best player?"

"Why don't you ask him," she snorted.

As a child player, I felt a certain kinship to Helen Sobel. Not in ability, of course, but in her early career she often benefited from her good looks. Men tried to take advantage of her at the bridge table, overbidding in the expectation that the "dumb blonde" would blow the defense. They soon learned better. As a youngster, I encountered adults who assumed they could pull the wool over my eyes. I enjoyed this built-in edge until I won the national tournament in Washington and began to shave.

Tournaments of that era often awarded trophies. That practice was downgraded to S & H green stamps, and now it's just masterpoints with a few notable exceptions, such as the Bermuda Regional, which bestows handsome local paintings on the winners of main events. The most prestigious championships still boast an ornate cup, such as one donated by Harold S. Vanderbilt.

The most prized trophy in my collection comes from a tournament in 1962 at Sacandaga, a resort in upstate New York. For years, it was a popular summer retreat for New York experts—it was at Sacandaga that I played with Kaplan and Sheinwold. My partner in the two-session Non-Life Master Pairs was my mother, Alice Boehm, and we won. What made it most memorable was a remark made by a fellow competitor, congratulating us. He looked at Alice, "You and your brother play so well together." As far as Mom was concerned, we could have finished dead last and the tournament would have been a giant success.

Jan Stone was my other female partner in that era. She was the wife of the Terrible Tobias who had developed her into a first-class player on the woman's circuit. She was strikingly beautiful, no surprise considering that she was a former television personality, "Janice the Paying Teller" on the quiz show, *Beat the Clock*. Since I had read and learned the Roth-Stone system and was a bit of a novelty, Jan came up with an idea.

The producer of *Championship Bridge With Charles Goren*, which ran nationwide from 1959–1962, asked Jan to appear, and she could choose her partner. This was the last year of the series, and the show, perhaps to prop up sagging ratings, had begun to invite celebrity athletes and actors who happened to play a little bridge. The contestants shuffled and played deals off-camera. The most interesting deals were chosen to televise, with the contestants reenacting their bids and plays before the camera. Alex Dreier, a prominent newscaster, was the narrator, representing the average player, and Goren provided expert commentary. The pair who scored the most points received a cash prize and continued the following week against new challengers.

Jan proposed me as her partner. She assured the producer that I was a capable player and mature beyond my years. He was satisfied and a weekend date was set, so as not to interfere with school. Jan and I would fly to Chicago where the show was filmed, and my excitement was barely contained. Then, with a month to go, Jan called to say that the deal was in jeopardy. The advertiser suddenly got cold feet, fearing that it would look unhealthy for its image if a minor participated in a format that involved gambling. Jan was so incensed at the Puritan morality behind the decision that she declined to participate. If she couldn't have me as her partner, the show couldn't have her telegenic self. The advertiser wouldn't budge, neither would Jan, and the show had to find another pair. My disappointment was profound but so was my respect for Jan Stone and her principled stand.

The reader may have the idea that my whole life was bridge. Not at all. My father knew the addictive hold bridge can exert, and there was never any question that my priorities were school, music, and athletics. Bridge was relegated to weekends and school vacations. In high school, during the academic year, I took a weekend job preparing boards for Bill Root's classes. Bill was a high-profile teacher, as well as an expert player and author.

Bill's lessons featured a lecture on a theme, followed by four illustrative deals that the students would play. His classes were large and profitable, and he found it both boring and time-consuming to prepare the deals. He offered me the job to pick up the boards Friday evening at his apartment and return them by Sunday.

Often, there were nearly 100 boards to prepare, and they were heavy to carry. I didn't want to blow a significant portion of my starting salary (15 cents per board) on taxis, so I carried them in their big, black boxes, sometimes more than a mile each way. At home, I studied the hand diagrams to determine how the students were expected to bid and play, how the deals related to the theme, and how each player was given a chance to shine. Much later in my life these experiences were to bear fruit. In high school, it was a way to earn money, usually while listening to classical music. I remember farming out some of my work to one of my younger sisters, Barbara, paying her a nickel a board. This experiment came to an abrupt end when my parents discovered the arrangement, which they somehow deemed exploitive.

CHAPTER 3

THE COLLEGE YEARS:
THE TUMULTUOUS 60's

Icontinued my schooling at Columbia, where I majored in music and minored in bridge. During my first week at a required class in calculus, with perhaps a couple of hundred students, not more than a couple of seats away sat a Texan named John Bromberg. He introduced himself in his pronounced Dallas drawl and explained that he had read the "College Bridge" section in the ACBL *Bridge Bulletin* magazine, summer of 1964:

A BRIDGE FAMILY

It is a rare privilege for a young bridge enthusiast to have an expert for a partner. Or, to put it another way, it is a rare pleasure for an expert to have a good partner as his child. One family who enjoys this distinction is that of Life Master George Boehm and his son, August. Although he is not yet eighteen, Augie is a veteran of tournament bridge. He won the National Teenage Championship in 1961 with Michael Becker (son of expert B. Jay Becker). Augie has enrolled at Columbia University and—if he can find a good partner—Columbia will fare very well in their intercollegiate competition during the next four years.

*

[*Author's note:* An accurate prediction, given a peer partner and strong teammates.]

31

John and I instantly formed a partnership that lasted through our four years at Columbia. More important, we became lifetime friends. The Columbia bridge club had been founded by Roger Stern, a prominent young bridge expert and attorney. In the duplicates on Wednesday evenings, we quickly made our mark. The captain of the college team invited us to participate in a match against the varsity, which included Jim Becker, who became well-known in the world of bridge, both as a player and a successful club proprietor. John and I auditioned well and were allowed to join the team; when the varsity graduated the next year, John became club president and we chose our own team.

Our foursome was composed of Allan Hillman from Baltimore and Richard Margolis from Milwaukee, a pair John christened the Aviary. This was partly due to their physical resemblances to a crow and a goose, plus a propensity to "fly around the room" when they squabbled over their occasional bad result. The Aviary remained tethered, John became a Life Master playing tournaments in Texas over the summers, and our team prospered, winning many intercollegiate titles.

Our team had set lineups, but team captain John still had to make executive decisions. One winter weekend, we journeyed to Keene, New Hampshire to play a match against Dartmouth. It was snowing heavily, and the single-engine prop plane barely made it. Our Dartmouth opponents picked us up at the airport and drove us to their campus. We sat down to play, and at halftime we were ahead by a staggering amount.

Captain Bromberg called a team meeting. "Boys, there are only a couple of flights per week in and out of Keene. The flight tomorrow (Sunday) is the last until mid-week. There are no taxis to take us back to the airport. We depend on our opponents' kindness to drive. Please, please, let them win back some imps."

We did, they did, and by Sunday evening we were safely ensconced in New York.

At graduation, John, Allan and I received Merit Awards from the Alumni Association for bringing glory to Alma Mater (Richard, now christened the Penguin, received his the following year when he graduated). The glory was partly due to collegiate bridge victories but also to fairly frequent appearances in *The New York Times* bridge column, then written by Alan Truscott. Some columns described matches that we organized against distinguished bridge alumni, such as the first one against John Solodar, Roger Stern, and George Boehm, among others. That first year, the alumni defeated our varsity; the next year, the varsity turned the tables.

Alan Truscott was a booster of youth in bridge. He himself had started young, and he knew that the world of bridge depended on revitalizing itself, as would any organized activity. Within a decade, the ACBL would lose sight of this essential need, but that is another story to be covered in a later chapter.

Alan wrote in his column of October 20, 1966, that our Columbia student team had narrowly beaten a team of four distinguished alumni. Whether this was a sign that the younger generation would become more highly skilled than their forebears was left an open question, but, in any event, in a tight 20-board match our college group defeated Mrs. Carlyn Brall, Sam Fry Jr., Richard Kahn, and Lee Hazen by 3 imps. Since the three men had all recently represented the United States in Bermuda Bowl competition, we felt a sense of accomplishment. We could play on a par, at least in the short run, with genuine experts.

Our foursome took academics seriously. John and Allan were pre-law; Richard was pursuing two degrees, one at Columbia, the other at the nearby Union Theological Seminary, preparatory to becoming a rabbi; and I, a music major, concentrated on piano on the side, since Columbia did not provide instrumental training.

Bridge escapades were never too distant, though. One of our after-hours haunts was the Chess and Checker Club of 42nd Street. That's how it was listed in the phone book; denizens knew it as "The Bucket of Blood" (also known as "The Fleahouse"). This was the era when 42nd Street was populated with seedy movie houses, peep shows, pornographic bookstores, pimps and prostitutes. None of these deterred us; in fact, this was an important part of the rounded education that only a big-city university can provide.

The entrance to the establishment was on the ground floor. You walked up a flight of stairs, which was often soaked with urine from the drunks and homeless. On the second-floor landing, a large set of rooms opened up, revealing table after table where all sorts of games were being played. There was chess, checkers, backgammon, Scrabble, go (a complex Asian board game), bridge, and a couple of games that were invented at "The Bucket" and understood only by the inventors.

A proprietor stood at the cash register. If you wanted to play, you paid a fee on the way out based on the time spent. This was the house's cut; if you wanted to gamble, that was your business. I don't remember Allan's spending time there, but John, Richard and I passed many hours on weekend nights when we probably should have been dating. We played set games; that is, we kept the same partner throughout a challenge match. "The Bucket" bridge players were a motley crew. Some played their cards well, but their bidding had no science, and they hadn't learned the key element of bridge: partnership trust.

The luck of the deal makes bridge a poor gambling choice. Couple that with the need to rely on partner, and one quickly realizes that solo games like gin, poker, and backgammon give the skilled individual a better chance to come out ahead. Still, we tended to win at "The Bucket" and, to such an extent, that toward the end of our college careers we couldn't find a game. Their bridge players wouldn't play us.

One evening, a Columbia friend named Jeff Lockshin and I ventured to "The Bucket." Jeff played a little bridge, but he knew he wasn't varsity material. At "The Bucket," I tried to interest the loungers in a set game, but I got no takers, even though I explained that Jeff was strictly an amateur. I doubt they believed me, every one of them was a hustler himself. Finally, a guy named Asa said, "As long as you're here, why don't you play a different game. Try Scrabble; you two college boys should know plenty of words."

Jeff and I inquired what sort of match Asa was proposing. "I'll let you consult. We don't play for very high stakes."

What about the chess clocks that the Scrabble players also used? "I'll set my clock for five minutes," said Asa.

"Per move?"

"Per game. If I exceed five minutes, you win. You can take half an hour."

Well, we were young and a bit green, but we knew a hustle when we heard it. Jeff and I retired to a corner, counted our cash, and decided we could afford what was coming. By the way, one element of Bucket Standard was to purchase two subway tokens at Broadway and 116th Street. That way, if "The Bucket" cleaned you out, you could return to campus. Bridge players call that a safety play.

In Bucket Scrabble, your clock was running while you were thinking. When you made a play, you had to total your score and punch the clock to stop your own and start the opponent's. Asa played at the speed of light, and the match quickly became lopsided as Jeff and I plodded behind. In the middle game, as the board was becoming crowded, Asa made a combination play that involved the word "rotl." We had never heard of such a word and decided to challenge. In Scrabble, the challenger looks up the word in the dictionary. If the word exists, the play counts and the challenger loses his next turn. If the word isn't in the dictionary, the play is canceled and the challenged player loses a turn.

Rotl is a Middle Eastern weight. Asa's play counted, we lost a turn, and the margin mounted. Towards the end of the game, Asa made another combination play, this time involving "artal." We figured he might be bluffing since we had already lost a challenge, and we challenged again.

"It's *your* funeral," he said grimly.

We found "art," "artel," but not "artal." "Nice try," we grinned.

"You're not looking in the right place. Look under 'R.' "

"R?"

"Look under 'rotl.' "

Sure enough, the plural of rotl is artal. Asa finished the game with a flourish, still well under five minutes, and we totaled the damage. Between what we lost to Asa and the time fee to "The Bucket," we were nearly cleaned out, but what an education. At Ivy League tuition rates, it was cheap. Asa allowed that he wasn't the best Scrabble player at "The Bucket," but he knew most words of seven letters or less in the *Funk & Wagnalls Unabridged Dictionary*, and he was working on the eights.

An experience like this gives one a sense of Olympian standards. And it is a reminder not to make stern judgments based on superficialities.

*   *   *

One final "Bucket" story with a moral: On Thanksgiving eve in 1968, I had graduated from Columbia and Richard was still enrolled. We hadn't seen each other in a while, so we met for dinner in midtown, caught up, and decided to venture to the nearby "Bucket." The Damon Runyon cast of characters greeted us as long-lost brothers and instantly accepted our challenge to a set game. They rotated partnerships while ours remained intact. Starting about 9 p.m., we played until sunrise the next morning. Our opponents, Psycho Sam, Wendell the Banker, Freddie the Fish, The Man with the Hat, and others grabbed an early lead, but around 3 a.m. the cards turned in our favor.

In bridge, if you are dealt consistently poor cards, it is hard to utilize your skills, particularly at rubber bridge where overtricks barely matter. Playing duplicate, a run of bad cards shouldn't diminish your chance of winning, because every other pair in your direction is dealt the same bad cards, and your results are compared to theirs. The players who lose the least with bad cards are the winners. Demon defense is the order of the day, and it is important to maintain concentration through a bad run. Richard and I knew this, we remained patient, and when the deals started to favor us, we made the most of our opportunities.

Our experience had taught us one extremely important lesson that I urgently pass along. Average, even average-plus players, tend to leap to premature conclusions, both in the bidding and on defense. Bridge is a game of collaboration, and experts constantly try to help each other solve problems. "The Bucket" players, proud of their individuality, were not constitutionally suited to partnership games, and the world of bridge abounds with similar types.

Remember Abe Schwartz's psych, playing money bridge with my father? From the inception of contract bridge until the 1950's, the science of bidding was rudimentary. Players thought of themselves as individuals more than pairs. Standard bidding was pretty much the same everywhere, first Culbertson's quick–trick evaluations, then Goren's point-count methods. The few conventions of the day were standardized, and a good player could sit down opposite another good player and expect few, if any, misunderstandings. Individual flair counted for more than partnership harmony, and, in such an environment, psychic bidding was in vogue. If you could put one over on an opponent, that's flair. If the deception left partner in the dark, no one worried too much. For instance, suppose you are dealt:

♠ 10 5 3 2 ♡ 7 ◇ Q 8 7 4 2 ♣ J 10 2

The opponents are vulnerable, you're not, and the auction goes pass — pass — ? to you. Pass is normal, but there was a day when experts might choose to open one diamond in their long suit or, even more exciting, one heart in their singleton! The idea was to bamboozle the opponents, who probably held the combined strength for game, even slam, given partner's pass. One heart might steal their suit. Suppose you psych one heart and partner responds one notrump; you pass and hope that neither opponent can act. Since both hold heart length, neither can make a takeout double and, on a good day, your partner goes down 50 per trick with the opponents cold for at least a vulnerable game. Of course, psyching could create a colossal disaster if partner puts you in four hearts, doubled and clobbered.

No single deal proves anything, but the long-term price of psyching is that partner begins to mistrust your normal bids. When you hold an authentic one-heart opening, in the back of partner's mind is the recollection that you sometimes psych, and he may twist himself into a pretzel trying to allow for the possibility. Routine contracts are missed, and the partnership fabric begins to fray.

The Kaplan-Sheinwold and Roth-Stone systems of the 1950's, with their highly detailed agreements, provided for controlled, lead-directing psychic openings, 2-6 points, thereby acknowledging ingrained expert habits. Later iterations of the systems discarded psychs. Partnership discipline became paramount, with both players adhering to their systemic agreements rather than indulging in flights of fancy or a seat-of-the-pants approach. Experts gradually adopted one of these systems or created systems of their own, and systemic players began to replace the go-as-you-please school.

The cornerstone of Kaplan-Sheinwold (K-S) is the weak no-trump; a one-notrump opening shows 12-14 points, balanced distribution. Balanced hands in this range are a lot more common than notrump openings with 16-18 (the prevailing range in the 1950's), perhaps two-and-a-half to three times more likely. This meant that K-S adherents opened one notrump much more frequently than other players, a substantial benefit, since one notrump is an easy opening to respond to, and it is more preemptive than the alternative opening of one club or one diamond on a minimum, balanced hand. K-S mandated five-card majors, another departure from the Goren standard, and the accompanying forcing response of one notrump. Inverted minor-suit raises, very popular today, were another part of K-S. The system has stood the test of time.

Roth-Stone (R-S) also stipulated five-card majors, the forcing one-notrump response, and the radical idea of very sound opening bids in first or second seat, at least 14 points. Many of the original R-S ideas have lost favor, but the negative double, introduced by R-S in 1957, is virtually universal. After an opening and an overcall, responder's double is takeout for the unbid suits. Formerly, such a double was pure penalty, or penalty-oriented.

The negative double was nicknamed Sputnik, the Russian satellite from the same year. To those who hailed the negative double, its space-age nickname suggested exciting new frontiers. To those who hated it because it upset the old order, Sputnik deserved its sinister, cold-war connotation.

Five-card majors, the forcing one-notrump response, and negative doubles are ubiquitous in today's tournament world; you probably play them yourself. In the 1950's, these chicks had just been hatched by the K-S and R-S system inventors. They didn't gain immediate acceptance; four-card majors and the nonforcing one-notrump response (6-9 points) lingered for decades. Bridge players are almost as resistant to change as the rest of the world.

A hard-earned lesson learned from the Italians provided a boost to scientific bidding. From the late 1950's and continuing for over a decade, the Italian international Blue Team dominated world play, a domain that the United States had called its own. The Bermuda Bowl, awarded to the World Champion team, never seemed to leave the shores of Italy during this era. The Italians had many great players, but so did other nations. The Blue Team played systemic bridge, and time and again their careful, detailed approach in the bidding carried the day. They never psyched and rarely preempted; instead, they relied on remorseless accuracy. Eventually, the rest of the world caught on, and today, it is inconceivable to find a top-flight pair that doesn't have a partnership notebook filled with hundreds of understandings. At that all-night session at "The Bucket" many years ago, Richard and I were just forming a partnership, but we both subscribed to disciplined, partnership principles. The lessons of the greatest players had not escaped us.

In bridge today, the proliferation of conventions (artificial calls that help describe a hand) is both a boon and a curse. Tournament players love to learn and tinker with conventions. If conventions are thoroughly understood, they improve accuracy. Forward-thinking players enjoy the intellectual activity of expanding their horizons. Teachers and writers love the modern trend, because it gives them something to lecture or write about.

However, the downside is that the highest level of tournament bridge has grown separate from the game the average player loves and plays. Big-time bridge would love to attract sponsorship and higher visibility, perhaps create a tournament circuit with substantial cash prizes and television coverage. The main problem is that big-time bridge has become too complex for the typical spectator to follow. Progress has also become the enemy.

*   *   *

Graduation Day at Columbia in 1968 nearly didn't take place. It wasn't lack of academic credits, although there were two potential obstacles. Any student with unreturned books to the library was prohibited from graduating, and all underclassmen had to pass a swimming test. Columbia was a bastion of liberal arts education, with required courses in art and music as part of the core curriculum. *Mens sana in corpore sano* (A sound mind in a sound body) was the classical ideal, and, at Columbia, if you couldn't swim two laps in the pool, you weren't allowed to graduate. Seniors were known to cram remedial swimming as graduation approached.

The spring of 1968 posed other problems. In April, a rebellious group of students (SDS, Students for a Democratic Society) stormed Dean Coleman's office and held him hostage. Other students invaded President Kirk's office and set up camp in his absence. Still others commandeered classroom buildings, and the entire university was shut down. The rebels objected to Columbia's involvement with Washington's war effort in Vietnam, a hotbed of contention on campus and around the nation. Columbia's alleged high-handed treatment of the community was another issue, as long-time local residents were dispossessed from single-room-occupancy buildings to make room for campus development.

The athletes, fraternities, and the ROTC (pre-military) opposed the rebels' goals and were incensed that a small group of dissidents could derail the functioning of a large institution (sound familiar?). Parents, who were footing big tuition bills, complained that their children were being deprived of an education. At long last, the administration reluctantly called upon the New York City police force to liberate the buildings from the rebel's hands. Ugly, violent scenes ensued as the cops stormed the campus through underground tunnels, cleared the buildings, and set up armed guard stations. Campus life was sufficiently disrupted that the administration decided to hold graduation exercises off campus, inside nearby St. John's Cathedral.

Upsetting as the disruption was, it was also educational. Students pitted against administration, liberals versus conservatives, youth versus establishment, the faculty all the while attempting to mediate, and the vigorous police action were a healthy antidote to an educational system that was sometimes criticized as being ivory tower, remote from reality. Rebellion against authority was hardly confined to Columbia; Berkeley and Paris witnessed similar protests, the sexual revolution and drugs made significant impacts worldwide, and the civil-rights movement and feminism were challenges to long-held traditional beliefs.

Meanwhile, my friends and I tried to maintain normalcy by attending whatever classes that could still be held off-campus, sometimes in professors' homes, even on a park lawn. Courses were graded on a pass-fail basis, and the academic process continued as best it could.

Deprived of a normal academic graduation, John Bromberg and I happened to have a most appropriate bridge graduation. New York held an annual regional tournament around Memorial Day. The main team event was the Reisinger Knockout, and John and I formed a team with my father and a partner of his, Pedro Cabral. Today, knockout team events saturate the tournament landscape. They are typically organized in brackets; your team's total masterpoint holding is computed, and you play in a bracket with seven other teams who have similar masterpoint totals. If you win one match, you are already in the semi-finals

BIG DEAL

and have earned a generous masterpoint award, although veteran players sneer at the term "earned."

The Reisinger of 1968 was a typical open tournament; novices competed against experts. The event was seeded, but masterpoints served as only a rough guideline. In New York, the enlightened seeding committee rated players on ability and recent tournament results, not on an accumulation of masterpoints which might simply reflect a long career. Our pair was too young to have garnered many points, and despite our veteran, expert teammates, our team was placed at the top of the unseeded group. For strange reasons, that year the top unseeded team (#33) played its first match against the top-seeded team (#1) instead of the usual bracketing of #1 vs. #64, #2 vs. #63, and so on. As a result, we faced the defending champions, all world-class experts in their primes.

The match of 32 boards was played in halves. For the first half, John and I sat down against John Crawford and Tobias Stone, not only two of the world's best, but players who were famous for intimidating gamesmanship, particularly Crawford. We managed to hold our own, and at the end of the half, after comparing scores, we were tied. Word spread rapidly that there might be an upset in the making, and the number of kibitzers seemed to double for the second half.

We enjoyed the challenge and limelight, and elected to play Crawford-Stone again. When we sat down at their table, Stoney immediately summoned the director, Harry Goldwater, a legend in his own right. When Goldwater arrived, Stone stated that the conditions of contest prohibited playbacks, that is, the same pairs opposing each other in consecutive segments. We would need to play at the other table, Stone insisted.

"Stoney, did your team exercise its seating rights for the first half?" asked Goldwater.

"Who cares. We're claiming our rights now."

43

"Sorry. If you didn't state your intentions at the beginning of the match, you are deemed to have chosen seating assignments for the first half. Your opponents have the choice for the second half."

"Goldwater, you must be the worst director in tournament history. You don't know a thing about conditions of contest."

"Really? I'm ruling that the boys may sit where they choose. What are you afraid of anyway, a couple of college kids?"

All this was entertaining for the throng of kibitzers, and we enjoyed it immensely.

As play progressed in the second half, it was clear that the match was still nip-and-tuck. We continued to hold our own against the champs. With only our side vulnerable, Crawford opened two spades in third seat, normally a weak-two bid with a decent six-card suit. John overcalled a sketchy three hearts, I bid a marginal four hearts, and we were in a game not reached at the other table. Stone lead a spade. Our spades were divided ace-third opposite three low. John won with the ace and proceeded to draw trumps with a winning finesse; Stone discarded a spade.

John smiled at Crawford, "You opened a five-card suit." A little later, as John was developing a side suit with another winning finesse, Stone discarded another spade. John chuckled, "Imagine that, he opened a four-card suit."

"You talk like a child," snarled Crawford.

"I am a child, but I'm about to make an impossible four hearts."

At the conclusion of the match, Stoney showed his class, "You boys played magnificently—you may have beaten us." We rushed to compare scores, but, alas, our teammates had suffered the worst of it, and we lost a squeaker. Still, after our initial disappointment, it dawned that we had acquired the ability to play against the very best.

Bridge diplomas awarded, *magna cum laude*.

Two years later, Crawford and Stone asked us to play on a team with them in the Reisinger, but John was attending law school in Austin, and we were forced to decline. The 1968 Reisinger was the last serious event where John and I played as partners. Geographical separation, career, and family obligations intervened. The Columbia foursome still meets for our personal reunions, and we remain in close touch. It's possible that, without bridge, our group would have maintained contact for five decades (and counting), but I rather doubt it, in part because such long-term relationships are so rare. What knits a group together is commonality, and living through the tumultuous Sixties on a vibrant campus while sharing a passion for an absorbing game has done the trick.

CHAPTER 4

POST-COLLEGE:
BRIDGE IS ON THE MARCH

The first article of mine that *The Bridge World* published was in 1969, and it is obviously connected to those final days on campus. It is reprinted here from the March 1969 issue.

COLLEGE BRIDGE IN THE CRYSTAL BALL
BY AUGUST W. BOEHM

At a Great American University, there came to be a difference of opinion. The students didn't care for the way the Administration ran the University; so in dissent—Campus Radical Style—they commandeered half the buildings.

The Faculty Committee hastily convened to arbitrate. Their determination: "Since reasonable negotiation is out of the question, let us arrange a contest to determine which side shall capitulate. Because the members of the Administration are advancing in years, a contest involving physical exertion, such as shuffleboard, seems inappropriate. A University is first and foremost an institution for scholarship. Therefore, we propose a game where the premium is placed on cerebration. Bridge, of course."

This conclusion was presented to both sides. Hotblood Dove, the student leader, leaped at it. "Just the thing. We'll confront them in an area which is directly connected with the Higher Middle to Lower Upper Class we oppose. In short, we'll beat them at their own game."

University President Hiram Throckmorton was equally enthusiastic. "Perfect. What we'll do to them at the card table will prove to the world that those young whippersnappers aren't worth the ashes of their Selective Service registration cards."

To minimize luck, the contest was set up as a team-of-four match, imp scoring, 24 boards. (Explaining the comparative brevity of the match, considering the stakes involved, a Faculty spokesman commented: "The less the major protagonists are in direct confrontation, the greater the likelihood of non-violence.")

On Boards 1-23, the Administration built up a lead of 14 imps. Their seasoned bidding and common-sense judgment had offset the youngsters' skillful card play and flair, with something to spare. On Board 24, the cards were dealt as follows (directions shifted for convenience):

North dealer
Neither side vulnerable

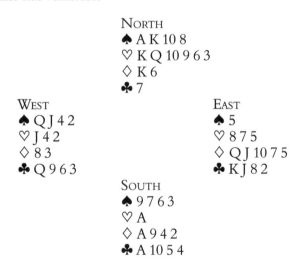

NORTH
♠ A K 10 8
♡ K Q 10 9 6 3
◇ K 6
♣ 7

WEST
♠ Q J 4 2
♡ J 4 2
◇ 8 3
♣ Q 9 6 3

EAST
♠ 5
♡ 8 7 5
◇ Q J 10 7 5
♣ K J 8 2

SOUTH
♠ 9 7 6 3
♡ A
◇ A 9 4 2
♣ A 10 5 4

When the deal was first played, the students reached six spades from the North seat. The members of this pair had spent their Junior year abroad at the Sorbonne, where they had learned the latest riot techniques and canapé. Thus, the opening bid from North had been one spade, in accordance with the principle of bidding the shorter suit first on two-suited hands. Many esoteric bids later, the boys lodged in the small slam. The diamond-queen lead was won with the ace, a top spade cashed, and the heart suit unblocked. When the nine of spades made a round trip, declarer drew the penultimate trump from West and ran his hearts. The defense could come to only one trump trick. But at the table where Hotblood Dove was West and President Throckmorton was South:

North	*South*
1 ♡	1 ♠
3 ♠	4 ♣
4 ♡	6 ♠
Pass	

After the more pedestrian path shown, Hotblood Dove was on lead in the West seat. "What has this archaic auction told me?" he mused. "That four-heart bid was made in the tone that shows a long suit, not a control." (Hotblood had played the game before.) "Declarer can't be missing too much in high cards, considering my trump holding. The best chance seems to get two trump tricks. If a safety play position exists, I'm simply going to have to talk the old fogey out of making it." This reasoned, Hotblood plunked down the jack of hearts.

President Throckmorton surveyed the dummy. "Curious lead," he thought. "Why did that young scamp lead a heart instead of the unbid suit? He's not so stupid as to lead from doubleton jack—in three years at my University he must have learned something—so I guess it's a singleton." The President scooped up the trick, tried a trump to the ace, returned to his hand with a diamond, and led a second spade. Dove ducked smoothly.

"I can just hear the sarcasm from the Board of Trustees if I lose to a doubleton honor, and East returns a heart for the over-ruff." Up went the king, and down went the contract. "I was afraid I had taken too long to lead," snickered Dove to his partner. "If I had been declarer, I would have reasoned that it wouldn't have taken my opponent twenty seconds to lead a singleton. I wouldn't have allowed myself to be deluded by such a shallow ruse." President Throckmorton had to be restrained. The swing exactly erased the 14-imp margin. Alas, the Faculty Committee had forgotten to make provisions for a tie. An on-the-spot attempt to settle the number of boards for a playoff ignited a heated and fruitless debate. The game broke up with relations between Administration and students greatly exacerbated. And so, unfortunately, it proved impossible to bridge the generation gap.

*   *   *

Meanwhile, the Spring and Summer of 1968 remained tumultuous; it was the year that most shaped us baby boomers. Besides campus protests and widespread unrest, two devastating assassinations occurred. Martin Luther King was shot dead in April, and Robert F. Kennedy in June, and the combined effects left the nation reeling. What was happening to the Stars and Stripes? Had our world gone crazy?

In the autumn of 1968, in New York City, the United Federation of Teachers conducted a strike, shutting down the public schools for about two months. This hardly resonated with national magnitude, but it affected a large number of recent college grads, such as myself, who were applying for jobs in the New York City public school system.

The New York teachers' strike in 1968 was a product of the times. Parent groups in ghetto schools were clamoring for greater influence in the educational process, and the teachers' union wanted no such interference. The racial riots in Watts of 1965, the recent assassination of Dr. King, and anti-war protests during the Democratic National Convention in Chicago in August, 1968 all helped fuel a tinderbox of mistrust and resentment between races, between young and old. When the community school board of Ocean Hill–Brownsville, a black ghetto in Brooklyn, dismissed a group of white teachers and administrators, the teachers' union demanded their reinstatement. Battle lines were drawn.

Totally untested, we were plunged into this maelstrom with a six-week crash course in education, culminating in a provisional teaching license. In autumn, we were assigned to fill the ghetto vacancies, guaranteeing an outcome that could only make matters worse. Where the strongest, most-experienced educators were needed, rookies were sent instead. On top of it, there were picket lines which we, the rookies, crossed. The schools, staffed by principals and assistant principals, were open for business. Most union teachers, but not all, refused to cross picket lines. We crossed, since we were not yet eligible to become union members; nonetheless, we were subjected to very un-Ivy League abuse.

Eventually, the strike was settled, and I managed to finish the academic year in one piece. Surviving was more a psychic hazard than a physical one, although there was a day when a disgruntled mother held the school principal and his secretaries at bay with an iron pipe, and another occasion when I was bitten by a teenage girl. The school year ended on a wry note connected to the annual Reisinger Knockout Team event.

In the 1969 Reisinger, I partnered my father, and we played with two other pairs. A team was often composed of six players (only four play at a time) to permit substitutions and accommodate scheduling conflicts. We didn't expect to go nearly as far as we did, the competition was fierce, but we won a succession of very close matches against highly-ranked teams and made it all the way to the final, where we lost. Still, it was great experience playing against a steady succession of established or up-and-coming experts.

There can be no better training, then or now, than to play head-to-head against experts in a long match. You are consistently challenged in the play. At the club level, if you misplay or misdefend, very often a less-than-expert opponent hands the contract right back to you. Against top experts, expect to pay for your mistakes. Club players don't create as many problems for you in the bidding, and the swindles you get away with at the club usually won't work against experts.

*   *   *

Back in Spanish Harlem at my day job, I had already decided to quit at the end of June and take my chances with the military draft. Accordingly, I used my full allotment of sick days, and as the Reisinger progressed and we remained in contention, I decided to call in sick for a couple of days and catch up on sleep. The evening sessions were long and grueling, and there is no way to drift off to sleep when adrenalin is still pumping and bridge hands are cascading through your brain. Come Monday, I was back in the classroom, and the school principal sent word that he wanted to see me in his office.

"You must have been pretty sick to miss half a week."

"Yes, sir; a bad bug of some kind."

"Left you weak, did it?"

"Afraid so."

"But not too weak to make it to the finals of the big event and get your name in *The New York Times*."

Turned out that he was a bridge enthusiast who followed Alan Truscott's bridge column daily. When he read the results of the Reisinger knockout over his Monday morning coffee on June 11, 1969, I was busted.

Peter Leventritt and Howard Schenken, who had first captured this title as a pair in 1943, played a pivotal role in winning the event. (Schenken's victories went back to 1931.) Their teammates were Ronald Crown, Richard Kahn, William Passell, and Dave Strasberg.

In the final, the Schenken team beat my team by 43 imps. My teammates were George Boehm, Fred Dossenbach, Keith Garber, Danny Salkoff, and Jay Wendt. We had earned our way to the final by defeating four strong teams by the slim imp margins of 9, 3, 7 and 1 in earlier rounds. This string of upsets christened us as the "Cinderella" team.

Leventritt (East) was the star of this deal from the final:

West dealer
North-South vulnerable

NORTH
♠ A 10 6 2
♡ K J 10 7
♢ 10 5
♣ 10 8 7

WEST
♠ J 7 5 3
♡ 6 3 2
♢ 7 4
♣ 9 5 3 2

EAST
♠ K 9
♡ A 9 4
♢ A J 8 3
♣ Q J 6 4

SOUTH
♠ Q 8 4
♡ Q 8 5
♢ K Q 9 6 2
♣ A K

SOUTH	WEST	NORTH	EAST
——	Pass	Pass	1 ♢
1 NT	Pass	2 ♢	Pass
2 NT	Pass	3 NT	(All Pass)

West led the club deuce, influenced by the fact that in the Schenken Big Club system, East might need to open one diamond holding longer clubs than diamonds, because one club would have been artificial and strong. Sitting South, I won and started with a heart to dummy's ten. Leventritt correctly won, worried that I might switch to diamonds and develop nine tricks. He returned a low club; I won and led the king of diamonds, unblocking the ten from dummy. Here, Leventritt showed his championship mettle by ducking. I took my three heart tricks and advanced the diamond five. East climbed up with the ace and cashed two club winners, West winning the fourth round with the nine. A spade return established East's king for the setting trick.

If East had made the reflex play of taking the diamond king, he would have subjected himself to a squeeze. In the ending, after the defense cashed its clubs, when West shifted to a low spade, I would have risen with dummy's ace and run my three heart winners. East would be forced either to abandon his diamond guard or to discard the spade king. Leventritt's crucial duck of the diamond king destroyed the entry position for the squeeze.

I remember feeling pretty proud to have unblocked dummy's diamond ten, forecasting the impending spade-diamond squeeze, since the high cards were well marked. Unfortunately, Leventritt forecast it too.

*   *   *

In 1970, the first national Swiss team championship was staged, and it ushered in a change that altered the character of tournament bridge. Team events had always been less popular than pair games. Arranging foursomes was inherently more difficult, particularly for the weaker players who sought pairs on their level willing to slug it out against stronger players. Prior to Swiss, the team formats were knockout and board-a-match. Knockout is scored at International Match Points (imps), somewhat similar to rubber-bridge scoring; the winner of a lengthy head-to-head match advances to the next round, the loser goes home or enters a consolation event. Board-a-match is scored like matchpoints; if your team scores a net plus, you win the board and receive one point, with a net minus you lose the board and score zero, and an exact tie is worth a half-point to each team.

Imp scoring is forgiving, because overtricks are relatively insignificant. Board-a-match is demanding, because the smallest error can cost your team the board. In long knockout and board-a-match events, the cream rises to the top. A long head-to-head match reduces the impact of luck, and in board-a-match virtually every tiny mistake is costly. Experts loved long knockout matches and board-a-match, which tend to run true to form, but there are more average players than experts, and in the late 1960's, the average player was growing exasperated at not being able to win any masterpoints in team events.

Enter the Swiss-team format, a movement borrowed from chess tournaments, where you play teams that have a similar score to yours. The scoring is at imps, so small errors are often forgiven, and the matches are short, typically seven boards rather than 28 or more. The shorter the match, the greater the impact of luck. Consider this example of a seven-board match between a team of four experts versus four average players. Let's say that five of the boards are flat. A routine contract is reached with routine bidding, and the only chance for a swing is an overtrick (1 imp). On these five boards, the expert team picks up three overtricks over their average opponents due to superior technique. On the sixth board, the experts play and defend a part score contract better than their counterparts and win a small swing (4 imps). The experts now lead by 7 imps.

On the final board, the experts outbid their opponents and reach a six-heart contract that is a huge favorite to succeed, while their counterparts languish in game. However, the missing trumps split five-zero, and the slam goes down one; at the other table, the average team plays in four hearts, making five. The swing, depending on vulnerability, is either 11 or 13 imps to the average team. Either way, the weaker team has won the match, but which team played better? It's not even close. In a longer match, the better team has time to overcome the bad break and, assuming it plays up to form, rates to win about 90 percent of the time. But in a hit-and-run Swiss setting, the weaker team will win perhaps 35 percent of the time. Guess which format is more popular with the average player?

The ACBL saw the sagging attendance figures at team events in the late 1960's and embraced the Swiss experiment. It became an overnight success, largely replacing board-a-match. The popular bracketed knockout events today feature relatively short matches, 12 boards. All these developments have been great marketing. Attendance is up, players win more masterpoints at a quicker rate than ever before, and they have more tournament success stories to share with their friends. Swiss and bracketed knockout events offer instant gratification; if you win one short match, you are guaranteed some masterpoints.

Most sectional and regional tournaments today offer a potpourri of events for players at all skill levels. It is not uncommon for a multi-day tournament to boast 25-30 different events. Lots and lots of winners but, as W. S. Gilbert of Gilbert & Sullivan observed in *The Gondoliers*, "When everyone is somebody, then no one's anybody." I prefer the tournaments of yore, when there were just a few headline events, and both the events and the winners enjoyed a bright spotlight.

Formerly, the typical tournament schedule slated Men's and Women's Pairs. Today, there are no Men's Pairs. In 1984, Jill and Robert Blanchard filed a suit against the ACBL, claiming that gender-restricted events prevented them from qualifying together for Bermuda Bowl playoffs. Eventually, the ACBL reclassified all such events as Open. However, women's events continue on the tournament calendar. The Venice Cup, the equivalent of the Bermuda Bowl, was instituted in 1974. The idea was to provide women with a chance to win a world championship.

Such an arrangement clearly implies that the level of the best women is below that of their male counterparts, else why create a separate category? Today, there are women's and open championships, but nothing restricted to men. Most of the world's best women players opt to play in women's championships rather than open competitions. Their chance of winning increases, and today's widespread professionalism provides female pros with financial incentives to remain in the female pond (more on this topic later, in the chapter on Professionalism). The irony, though, is that the separation does women a disservice. Why shouldn't women play as well, or better, than men? Women take more lessons and have more leisure time to compete. One reason is that they rarely compete against the top men head-to-head in long knockout matches, the ultimate test of skill. Ask any expert, male or female, to compile a list of the 100 best players, and it will be at least 90-percent male. Rant if you like, and some women do, but it is an accepted fact. If the top women were to compete regularly against males who were as good or slightly better, wouldn't it strengthen the women's game and partnerships? That's hard to refute, but women facing off against each other in national and international championships has become a comfort zone and the norm.

It's not just women. Throughout tournament bridge, most of today's players seek comfort zones. Flighted and bracketed events insulate competitors from unwanted challenges. Bridge has emulated golf's handicapping system. More players can enjoy competing, which is a bonus. But the rewards of winning are diluted, and masterpoints are inflated. In all likelihood, the aging bridge population is a big influence. At a certain point in life, many people feel that they have been through enough challenges. They realize that their powers are diminishing, and a less competitive arena is desirable.

It's all very understandable, but as the bridge population has aged, the game has gone soft. True, the top players seem as strong as the best of yesteryear, the systems are better, and the average player's level has improved greatly. Indeed, that is the most noticeable difference between the eras. However, when the tournament environment heavily encourages competitions of rookies versus rookies, seniors versus seniors, and women against women, something is lost. It discourages personal growth.

*   *   *

In the early 1970's, I found myself teaching at a boys' private school in New York. I taught everything in grades five through nine except French, Latin, and music—the school had a renowned music program run by a great teacher—and I coached three sports: football, basketball, and baseball. I had played all three sports through high school, as well as golf on the side, so I was well acquainted with athletics. *Mens sana in corpore sano.* It was invigorating to teach bright youngsters in a non-hostile environment; no iron-pipe incidents, no one bit me. One of my students happened to be Michael Root, son of bridge-pro Bill Root, who was one of my earliest employers.

Toward the end of my five-year stay, I found myself giving an occasional bridge lesson at night. Word must have gotten around (perhaps from the Root family) that I had credentials. It may have helped that I was single and there were several divorced mothers. At this all-boys school, there were a number of faculty members with homosexual orientation, so the straight guys like myself were prime candidates. In any event, I gave some lessons and rather enjoyed it. It's nice to earn extra income from doing something you enjoy and feel competent to explain. In addition, teaching adults was a relief from enforcing classroom discipline. On the other hand, adult minds are less agile.

I was feeling a young, spry, 27 years old, except when I saw a reprint of a "College Bridge" article in April, 1974, from the ACBL's *Bridge Bulletin*. Note that the ACBL magazine still ran a feature about college bridge. Within a few years, the ACBL withdrew its coverage of youthful bridge. It was rumored that a Board member's child flunked out of school, and bridge was branded as the culprit. By adopting such a misguided Puritanical stance, the League lost a generation of young players, and it is desperately trying to catch up. In the 1950's and 1960's, bridge was valued among the young. There were many college-age players, and bridge functioned in an important social role. As other entertainment options came into existence, bridge was nudged towards the sidelines. It came to be associated with retirement communities or an indoor, less healthy sport. Some of this shift was inevitable, but the ACBL did itself much harm by treating the game as an undesirable activity for youths.

What gave me pause about the reprint was the title:

ANOTHER GOLDEN OLDIE

The following is as true today as it was when published in the *Bridge Bulletin* seven years ago:

With more and more students achieving high rankings in the ACBL tournaments, it is not unexpected to find that many college stars are also expert analysts. In particular, today's college competitors are adept at ferreting out unusual possibilities in either bidding or play.

This interesting deal [*See top of next page.*] encountered by Columbia's August Boehm and John Bromberg at a recent tournament also features a battle to establish a squeeze position.

The opening lead marked East with the club ace-king, so Boehm decided that the heart finesse (apparently his only hope) was a favorite to lose. With an ace and two kings to go with his spade void, East probably would not have passed originally, especially at favorable vulnerability.

However, declarer saw a further chance. The bidding indicated that East held five diamonds. If that defender also held the heart jack, he could be subjected to a squeeze. Boehm ruffed the club and played the ace-queen of hearts, ruffing West's king. He

East dealer
North-South vulnerable

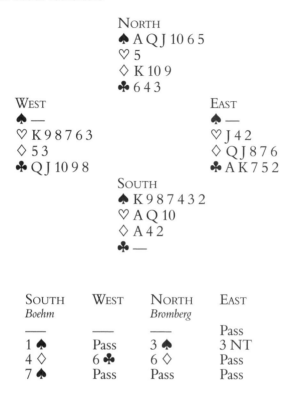

NORTH
♠ A Q J 10 6 5
♡ 5
♢ K 10 9
♣ 6 4 3

WEST
♠ —
♡ K 9 8 7 6 3
♢ 5 3
♣ Q J 10 9 8

EAST
♠ —
♡ J 4 2
♢ Q J 8 7 6
♣ A K 7 5 2

SOUTH
♠ K 9 8 7 4 3 2
♡ A Q 10
♢ A 4 2
♣ —

SOUTH Boehm	WEST	NORTH Bromberg	EAST
—	—	—	Pass
1 ♠	Pass	3 ♠	3 NT
4 ♢	6 ♣	6 ♢	Pass
7 ♠	Pass	Pass	Pass

Opening lead: Club queen

---

ruffed a club, returned to dummy with a trump to ruff the last club, then ran all of dummy's trumps, squeezing East in the red suits.

*

[*Author's note:* A dummy reversal plus a transfer squeeze was easy pickin's back then. Nowadays, it might take a little longer.]

*   *   *

In the summer of 1974, New York hosted a Nationals (now called North American Bridge Championships or NABC's), a rare event, because New York was widely perceived as expensive, rude, and dangerous. Native New Yorkers always resent these labels as dismissive of the big picture, even though each allegation bears some truth. What can't be ignored is that New York is one of the most significant cities on the planet, certainly in the bridge sense. It was customary for the host city to offer entertainment, and what was more natural than for New York to present a musical revue called *Bridge to Broadway*. Sandy Stern was the producer, Estee Griffin the head writer, and the cast featured New York bridge players who had background in song and dance, plus a few ringers from Actors' Equity. The Director was a professional actor with no bridge knowledge. Sandy Stern had to explain the jokes to him so he could stage the numbers.

One of the best was a brilliant parody by Estee Griffin of "Gee, Officer Krupke" from *West Side Story*, where members of the Jets gang satirize how they are viewed by society's various authoritarian figures.

(The first three speeches are spoken, the rest is sung.)

Arab:
What happened with your protest?

Action:
Protest! That's all people do around here. Somebody's always hollerin' cop—I mean Dy-reck-tor.

Krupke:
Yes—who called?

Action:
Dear Tournament Director, we ain't done nothin' wrong,
My partner, don't eject her because she took too long.
She had a little problem, she barely stopped to think,
Golly Moses, why make such a stink?

All:
Gee, Mister Director, it just isn't so,
He pulled her business double 'cause the tempo was slow.
We know we were damaged, so please fix our score,
Three diamonds doubled making four.

Action (indignant):
Making four?

All:
Making four, making four, well we could make four,
With a misdefense we would make four.

Krupke (spoken):
All right—three diamonds doubled making four.

(Stage business, leading to Action's appeal of the Director's ruling in front of the Tournament Committee.)

Action:
Dear Tournament Committee, just look here at my hand,
No one but Walter Mitty would let that double stand.
My partner always huddles, I'm givin' you no bull,
Leapin' Lizards, anyone would pull.

Baby John:
Oh, Mister Director, your ruling was right,
This creep took out the double 'cause he knew it was light.
Don't question his ethics, don't call him a thief,
He may turn over a new leaf.

(More business, moving the protest to the Tournament Recorder.)

Action:
Dear Tournament Recorder, why do you pick on me?
If I was out of order, I didn't mean to be.
Everybody huddles, so why crack down on us?
Glory-osky, why make such a fuss?

Arab:
Now Mister Recorder, we've got to be fair;
This slob may not be crooked, though he does have long hair
A one-year suspension should make him go straight,
Or do you think it is too late?

Krupke:
It's too late.

All:
It's too late, it's too late, it is much too late;
For a reformation, it's too late.

Baby John:
The trouble is he huddles.

Arab:
The trouble is he peeks.

Baby John:
The trouble is he muddles.

Arab:
The trouble is he speaks.

Baby John:
The trouble is he's winning.

Arab:
The trouble is he's won.

All:
Mister, all our troubles are undone.
Gee, Mister Director, our score's heaven-sent;
This way we'll top our section with a sixty percent. *
Gee, Mister Director, what are we to do?
Gee, Mister Director, wreck you!

* In 1974, lines 2 & 3 of the final stanza read, "Gee, Mister Director, please change our score. This way we'll top our section with a 184." The updated version (2004) reflects the impact of computer scoring.

That summer, I was booked to teach on a few cruises (more later) that conflicted with the rehearsal period. Accordingly, I was given a reduced role, a cameo part or walk-on part where I sang one song and left. The song, lyric by Harold Lillie, was based on "The Impossible Dream," which suited my bass-baritone range and timbre, and I was costumed in Don Quixote's full armor. On cue, I lifted the helmet's visor and sang:

To reach the unreachable slam,
To make the unmakable game,
To beat the unbeatable contract,
To play with a world-famous name.

This is my quest,
To play with the best;
And 'til it's accomplished,
I never will rest.

To fight for the right
To end up in first place,
To be willing to march into hell
For the masterpoint race.

And the game will be better for this,
That one man, new to fortune and fame,
Aspired with his last ounce of courage
To win in his first novice game. *

* Equivalent to today's Newcomer game

Alan Truscott showed off his musical versatility in spinning his *New York Times* column of September 14, 1974. He used this deal:

North dealer
East-West vulnerable

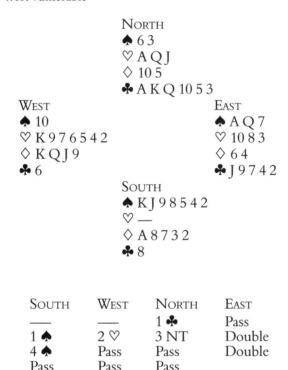

NORTH
♠ 6 3
♡ A Q J
◇ 10 5
♣ A K Q 10 5 3

WEST
♠ 10
♡ K 9 7 6 5 4 2
◇ K Q J 9
♣ 6

EAST
♠ A Q 7
♡ 10 8 3
◇ 6 4
♣ J 9 7 4 2

SOUTH
♠ K J 9 8 5 4 2
♡ —
◇ A 8 7 3 2
♣ 8

SOUTH	WEST	NORTH	EAST
—	—	1 ♣	Pass
1 ♠	2 ♡	3 NT	Double
4 ♠	Pass	Pass	Double
Pass	Pass	Pass	

Alan was a fan of Broadway musicals, as well as Gilbert & Sullivan and Flanders & Swann from his British heritage. He recognized song parodies from *Annie Get Your Gun, Cabaret,* and *Man of La Mancha,* and singled out the quest of Augie Boehm (South) to make an unmakable game.

In the auction, North, Edith Sacks, had an interesting bidding problem at her rebid. She rejected three clubs as an underbid, considering her hand's great playing strength. She contemplated a penalty double with an eye toward garnering a 500-point penalty from the vulnerable opponents. If she had doubled after a pronounced pause, could South ethically have taken the double out? As in *West Side Story*, South could have explained: "Dear tournament committee, just look here at my hand, no one but Walter Mitty would let that double stand." Mrs. Sacks, bidding what came naturally, jumped to three notrump.

East deduced that North was relying on a long club suit, so he doubled, since he had clubs stopped and partner had made a vulnerable overcall. When South (me) continued to four spades, he doubled again.

West led the diamond king. I was aware of the reason for East's double of three notrump, so I knew I couldn't take enough quick diamond discards with trumps at large. Hoping to preserve an entry, I ducked. If West had shifted to a club, it would have severed my link to dummy, but West, sensing no danger, continued with the diamond queen.

This left me in control: I led the spade king, allowing for the possibility that West held a singleton queen. When East won with the ace, he was helpless. With West out of trumps, there was no way to stop declarer from throwing his diamond losers on dummy's side-suit winners. The defense had to settle for two trump winners plus a diamond, and declarer scored his doubled game, unmakable against first-class defense.

East was Howard Schenken. Experts were once polled as to whom they would chose as a partner if the stakes were one's life—Schenken won by a vast margin. You may remember that his team had beaten mine in the Reisinger final a few years back. This was a little bit of sweet revenge.

*   *   *

It was great fun, the show was a hit and performed twice in a large ballroom before a capacity crowd. Those were the days before computer scoring. Directors scored by hand, and, with the great volume of players at a Nationals, it took over an hour for all the scores to be posted. This posed the perfect time frame to put on a show, with players a captive audience. When the Nationals next returned to New York City in 2004, I revived the show, updated some songs, and, once again, it was a big hit (more on that later).

In the 1970's, I still played tournaments with my father, but I was also developing a partnership with Michael Engel that lasted about fifteen years. We had a number of successes, always in team events. We didn't enter pair games, because we found knockout and board-a-match more stimulating. New York, where Swiss events had originated, hadn't yet jumped fully on the Swiss bandwagon; board-a-match was retained and well attended, because New York City has always had a high concentration of strong players. When a Swiss was held, it was a four-session, two-day event. The length of the event added integrity and limited the impact of luck.

I had branched out considerably from my Roth-Stone training, and Michael convinced me to open four-card majors and to adopt a British-influenced, Acol-like structure where one got in and out of the auction fast. For us, lots of jumps were limit bids, not forcing as under the prevailing trend. We also played some conventions that were effective and difficult to play against, such as Two-Way Two-Bids and Namyats (Stayman spelled backwards).

Namyats has become fairly common; a four-club opening (or overcall) shows a strong four-heart preempt, four diamonds does the same for four spades. When the Namyats partner ideally declares, e.g.: four diamonds — pass — four spades — all pass, the preemptive hand appears in the dummy, and the closed hand is basically unknown, complicating the defense. Namyats gives the partnership an extra way to preempt at the four-level. The tradeoff is that eight-card minor-suit preempts must be opened with something other than four of a minor. The price is worthwhile, because major-suit preempts are more effective.

Two-Way Two-Bids involve two-diamond, two-heart, and two-spade openings—they are either an Acol two-bid, about eight winners with length in the bid suit, or a weak two-bid with length in the next higher-ranking suit (clubs over spades). Thus, two diamonds is strong in diamonds or weak in hearts. The partnership has mechanisms to discover opener's intentions; for example, after two diamonds — pass — two hearts — pass, opener passes with a weak-two in hearts but bids on with a strong hand; three diamonds shows long diamonds, three clubs shows a strong minor two-suiter. This convention never gained popularity, in part because it was illegal to use in most pair games, considered too difficult to defend against. Nonetheless, it caught the attention of some of my teammates and other partners, who happily learned the method because it produced good results. New York City was very liberal in permitting unusual methods, and we were able to use Two-Way Two-Bids locally. This suited us fine, because we didn't play outside the city, except for representing the New York district at a NABC in the Grand National Teams.

The Precision System made its appearance in the early 1970's, in large part because its inventor, Charles Wei, a Taiwanese shipping magnate, sponsored successful young teams that won knockout championships at the highest level. As usually happens, other players, hoping to copy the success of these experts, adopted Precision.

The foundations of the system are weak notrumps and an artificial one-club opening, showing 16-plus points, any distribution. Because the openings of one diamond, one heart, and one spade are thus limited to 15 points, system practitioners can open light and still show a narrow range (11-15), much more compact than standard systems where the opening bid of one-of-a-suit encompasses 12-21, or an even wider range. This is one of a big-club system's main strengths; in general, the side that opens the bidding has an advantage, because opener's partner can often gauge the degree of fit (or misfit) and compete appropriately. Very sound opening bidders cede this advantage to their opponents.

The strong, artificial one-club opening is a mixed bag. When the opponents don't compete, the big clubbers have an extra level of bidding at their disposal (compared to standard two-club openings). To defend against big-club systems, Steve Robinson and Kit Woolsey devised CRASH, an acronym for a method where a double of one club shows two suits of the same Color (blacks or reds), one diamond shows two suits of the of the same RAnk (majors or minors), and one notrump shows two suits of the same SHape (the round suits are hearts and clubs; the pointed, spades and diamonds). When advancer (the intervenor's partner) bids a suit, that is defined as "pass or correct," intervenor moves on if the bid is not in one of his long suits—e.g.: after one club — double (blacks or reds) — pass — one diamond — pass — ?, doubler would pass with the red suits or bid (probably one spade) with the blacks.

Suppose the artificial one club is doubled, and advancer holds a weak hand with at least four-four in the minors. He should jump in clubs, to a level consistent with the vulnerability, knowing that intervenor will correct to diamonds with the red suits. The idea is to maximize the chance for preemption if advancer fits either of intervenor's suits. The preemption poses real problems for the big-club partnership, attacking its main weakness, the omnibus one-club opening. Opener has shown a strong hand, but not necessarily a monster like a standard two-club opening, one that could inflict a sizable penalty. The one-club opener has supplied no distributional description, and the bidding may already be at the three-level or higher when the auction returns to him. In bridge theory, thrust generates counterthrust.

In the early days, the Fishbein convention was a fairly popular defense against three-level preempts. After an opposing preempt (say three hearts), double was treated as penalty, and the next-higher suit bid (in this case three spades) was used for takeout. This convention never became popular among experts, because it deprived the intervenor of a useful natural overcall, and the artificial next-suit takeout precluded playing for penalties when advancer held a defensive hand. However, in the modern game, where many players preempt on dust, especially when not vulnerable, there is a (very) mild case to restore Fishbein to provide a direct-seat penalty double.

Traditionalists have always treated a double of a one-notrump opening as penalty. Modernists decided that a penalty double of a strong notrump (15-17) has little utility, and conventions designed to compete with a two-suited hand, such as DONT (Disturb Opponents' NoTrump) have become popular, where double is an artificial takeout. The wind may be shifting again, as players broaden the range of one notrump to include 14-point hands with a good five-card suit, sometimes less, and with nontraditional distribution. This treatment appeals to its practitioners, because one notrump has preemptive value, and responder's bidding is well-charted, with Stayman, transfers, and other conventions at the ready. When the one-notrump opener starts lowering the requirements, there is an increased chance of a significant penalty, so some experts have returned to the traditionalist fold and restored the penalty double of one notrump.

Thrust and counterthrust.

*   *   *

Complex conventions tend to be permitted in tournaments where one pair squares off against another for several boards, such as knockout or Swiss teams. In pair games, where you oppose each other for perhaps only two deals, it is considered unfair to force the opponents to improvise or develop a defense to an unfamiliar weapon. Complex conventions are disallowed in pair games, except at the highest levels, where the practitioners must provide a written, approved defense. This protective attitude of the ACBL is in stark contrast to tournament organizations in Europe, say, where experimentation has been encouraged.

Apropos conventions and bidding styles, it is clear that no system stands above the crowd. If one did, every good player would adopt the Holy Grail. In fact, there are a great many approaches, each with its adherents. The important thing is to pick a detailed system that suits your partnership's personality and tolerance for complexity, then learn it thoroughly. What does personality have to do with it? Some players are conservative by nature, while others are aggressive. Conservative players favor sound openings and overcalls and reasonably traditional preempts. Aggressive methods call for light initial actions and a preemptive style where anything goes, particularly when nonvulnerable. The conservative player aims to explore for the best contract. The aggressive player puts a premium on impeding the opponents. There are winning players on both sides of the equation.

No doubt influenced by my father's versatility—for a lark, he sometimes used whatever methods his opponents' announced they would use—I have played Roth-Stone, Acol, a home-grown big-club system, Eastern Scientific, and Two-Over-One, all of which have merit, but none more unusual than Churchill. Consider this excerpt from *The Bridge World*, May 2002.

THE WISDOM OF THE SAGES
BY AUGUST W. BOEHM

What if your partner insisted that you do without Stayman, Blackwood, any forcing opening bid, and preempts? Bizarre? Not if that partner was the late S. Garton Churchill, "Church" to his legion of friends and admirers but always "Churchie" to his daughter, Barbara Thompson. Church, a Wall Street lawyer, was one of the winning players in the early days of contract bridge. In 1948, he won the National Masters' Pairs for the second time, with a record-breaking percentage. His bidding ideas were hotly debated, not least because they were considered maverick. As the decades advanced, his Non-Convention Card, listing all the conventions he did not employ, became a small tome. Yet, his ideas on bidding attracted a number of top New York experts, among them Paul Heitner, Alan Messer, and Roger Stern. In the early 1960's, Heitner wrote a fine article for *The Bridge Journal* describing Churchill's ideas. Do not think that because Church spurned conventions that he lacked a method. In fact, the Churchill style was carefully considered, a matter of timing the auction. Heitner cites this example:

WEST	EAST
♠ A J x x x	♠ x x
♡ A K x x x	♡ x x x x x
◇ K Q x	◇ A x x
♣ —	♣ x x x

Heitner and John Lowenthal, using their then-hypermodern Canary Club, reached the excellent six-heart slam. Hoping to demonstrate the system's effectiveness, Heitner presented this combination to Church and a regular partner, who produced this sequence:

Opener	*Responder*
1 ♠	1 NT
3 ♡	4 ◇
5 ◇	5 ♡
6 ♡	Pass

One notrump was the hallmark "utility" response, showing less strength than one-and-a-half essential tricks but a reason to respond. (A critical difference between Churchill and Standard is that with a weak hand and a long suit, a Churchill responder will bid one notrump even if the suit could be shown at the one-level.) The combination of four diamonds then five hearts indicated a concentration in diamonds and long but weak hearts. Note the modernity: the artificial one-notrump response and picture bidding. These cornerstones of the Churchill style long predated the Kaplan-Sheinwold and Roth-Stone systems. A useful corollary of the utility response is that after a new suit response (at least one and a half essential tricks), a change of suit by either partner is a one-round force. Thus, one heart — one spade — two clubs is forcing, which significantly reduces a recurring problem in Bridge World Standard when opener is dealt the likes of:

♠ A J ♡ A K x x x ◇ x x ♣ A Q x x

there is no need to overbid with three clubs or to misbid with two notrump, and no risk of being stranded prematurely in two clubs.

During my early twenties, I played successfully with Church for a brief span. (We won a two-session board-a-match in New York, one of the toughest events on the tournament calendar.) The experience was cleansing; everything depended on judgment and developing a sense of his style. Aside from the utility one-notrump response and an opening weak notrump—very pure:

$$\spadesuit \text{A Q x x} \quad \heartsuit \text{x x} \quad \diamondsuit \text{Q x x} \quad \clubsuit \text{A J x x}$$

wouldn't qualify, because it was too suit-oriented—there were no systemic buttons to push, no formulas to invoke woodenly. Hand evaluation was critical; one developed sensitivity to distribution, suit texture, and honor location—Church disdained point-count. He loved the 5-4-3-1 pattern, because of its special combining potential. Another Churchillian characteristic was very sound vulnerable overcalls. He would often pass, waiting for the opponents to limit their hands, before backing in, like Al Roth. Table presence and flair were necessary skills when playing with Church. If you possessed them, partnering him honed them.

During the late 1960's and early 1970's, the International Bridge Academy organized worldwide bidding contests in a format not unlike "Challenge the Champs." In 1969, Church entered with Alan Messer and left a record of their participation. A high qualifying-round score entitled them to compete in the final, to face 50 challenging combinations. They finished 13th out of 33 finalist pairs from the U.S.A. Church, whose standards were Olympian, was displeased with his result but happy to see that two members of his Table Cloth Club (a lunch-plus-bidding-discussion group) finished ahead of him: Bill Passell and Roger Stern, whose partner was Jeff Rubens.

Describing the final, Church wrote: "The problems were all beautiful and many, many of them were very tough indeed, but the correct answers were available to any partnership willing to play an intelligent style and to think while playing it."

Church was then 69 years young, wistful but determined, noting: "I am still hopeful that, before I die, I can find a partner who will really believe that I know what I'm talking about when it comes to the bidding and can once again have a bang-up game."

I've chosen a sprinkling of deals to illustrate Churchill's style and personality. The successful auctions will look familiar to today's experts, but in 1969 fewer pairs played systemically, and those systems were not as thoroughly developed. From the late 1930's, the infancy of contract bridge, Church was as dedicated to scientific bidding as anyone today, if by scientific we mean a thorough exploration of possibilities.

Appreciate these sequences:

West	East
♠ K 7 2	♠ A Q 6 5
♡ Q J 4	♡ A
◇ K	◇ A J 10 8 6 4 3
♣ A Q 9 8 6 3	♣ 2

Messer	Churchill
1 ♣	1 ◇
2 ♣	2 ♠
2 NT	3 ♡
4 ◇	6 ◇
Pass	

Score: 20/20. Commentary: "Bidding beautiful, particularly Alan's four diamonds over my three-heart move."

WEST	EAST
♠ 2	♠ A 6 5 3
♡ A K 10 9	♡ Q 7 5 3
◇ A K 9 8 2	◇ Q 7 4
♣ A J 6	♣ Q 5

Churchill	*Messer*
1 ◇	1 ♡
2 ♣	2 ◇
3 ♡	3 ♠
6 ♡	Pass

Score: 20/20. Commentary: "Isn't this a nice deal? The one-round force of two clubs allowed responder to give opener one of the two keys (two diamonds), and the game-forcing slam suggestion of three hearts made it easy for responder to give opener the crucial key."

WEST	EAST
♠ 9 2	♠ A Q J 10 3
♡ Q J 10 5	♡ A 8 7 6 2
◇ A K	◇ J 7
♣ A 10 7 3 2	♣ 4

Churchill	*Messer*
1 ♣	1 ♠
2 ♡	3 ♠
3 NT	5 ♡
6 ♡	Pass

Score: 20/20. Commentary: "Just getting too damn good!"

Church's two-heart reverse was permissible, because of the positive one-spade response. Note Messer's "quality" jump to three spades before inviting slam, isolating the diamond problem, which underscores the importance of productive sequencing.

Surely, deals like these are worth revisiting. All bridge theorists attempt to solve similar problems, and in constructive bidding Church was supremely gifted. How ironic that an ardent naturalist was at heart a scientist, albeit a scientist without conventions.

In 1979, a lengthy book was privately published by Church. From Edgar Kaplan's introduction: "Churchill's early auction gives the soundest of foundations to build later slam auctions, and the test of any system is how well it does in hitting the most difficult targets: slams. The Churchill method never attained popularity, probably because of the strong tide of artificiality that set in during the 1950's . . . The winds of fashion may shift. Players may once again put more faith in, and find more beauty in, a delicate deduction than a complex convention."

When you sat opposite this distinguished gentleman dressed in his emblematic three-piece suit, watch fob and chain, you were facing an artist who possessed a unique view of the landscape.

*   *   *

Teaching bridge, though not yet a pastime, was already a passport to leisure. In my early twenties, I was introduced to Harold Ogust. Harold had taken over the reins of the Goren empire, which included a daily syndicated newspaper column, books by Goren, and Travel With Goren, an enterprise that included contracts to staff cruise ships with bridge instructors.

Harold offered me my first cruise assignment in 1969, which led, directly or indirectly, to about seventy-five more. The terms were easy to swallow: an outside cabin, three or up to seven meals a day with good caviar on demand, and a liquor discount when drinks were already steeply discounted—the cruise lines hadn't yet made the bar a profit center. The duties were to lecture for one hour in the morning and run a duplicate and/or party bridge for about two hours in the afternoon, but only when the ship was at sea. When the ship was in port and during all evenings, your time was your own. My early cruises took me to Bermuda and the Caribbean. Later, I traveled to Mexico, Alaska, Europe, Russia, and the Far East. I wasn't asked to pay a fee to Travel With Goren, as was common with other subcontractors. I could bring a companion, and the only concerns were to avoid sunburn and not to put on weight.

The level of bridge on board tends towards the dismal, except for cruises specifically billed as bridge cruises, where a large segment of the passengers are dedicated tournament players. On the Goren regular cruises that I staffed, bridge was simply one of many activities the shipping line offered, there were fewer bridge players, and many participants were social players, hence the need to provide party bridge.

Anyone who has taught bridge on board has stories to tell. Here are a few of mine.

The first day at sea, I was lecturing and noticed an attractive young couple in attendance, actually taking notes. Only serious students take notes, and on vacation, most don't. The next morning, they were missing, but I ran into them at the lunch buffet line.

"I was surprised not to see you this morning. You seemed quite interested yesterday."

"Oh yes, bridge is very interesting. This morning, we learned backgammon."

When directing a duplicate on land, I like to locate North geographically, if possible. Some players seem to find it curiously stabilizing—duplicate bridge can make players very nervous, so any little thing helps. One afternoon, an old salt watched me distribute the table guide cards.

"Son, you're not doing it right. North is a compass point."

"I know, but on a rolling ship in the middle of the ocean, how can I tell from inside a ballroom which way is true north?

He smiled. "When in doubt, I'd make North the bow of the ship."

Speaking of rolling seas, on the first night out, the Cruise Director was welcoming the passengers at the after-dinner show. In that spirit, he instructed everyone how to play a game he had devised which he billed as a great ice-breaker. Passengers were invited to get up and dance, preferably with a stranger whom they had just met. The band would play, and when the Cruise Director called out the name of a drink, the dancers must react. "Scotch" meant switch partners to the left, "Bourbon" meant switch partners to the right, and "Gin" meant stop dancing. Anyone who failed to follow directions was eliminated, the rest remained on the floor. There was champagne for the winners.

The band started and after a few moments the Cruise Director cried "Scotch." Most dancers reacted appropriately, but a few got confused and they had to return to their seats. A few more rounds of "Scotches" and "Bourbons" thinned out the dance floor. "Gin" was the next instruction. Some couples stopped on cue, but others lurched when the ship hit a wave.

"You're out," the Cruise Director bellowed.

"But the ship rolled. How can you stand still on a moving dance floor?"

"Doesn't matter; you're out. Someone escort them off the floor immediately."

So much for putting people at their ease.

On Cunard ships, bridge players tended to gravitate towards their own kind. The British partnered each other, as did the Americans. Other nationalities were left to pair themselves. In part, this may have been xenophobic, but there were sound bridge reasons. The Brits speak a different bridge language from Americans. They play weak notrumps, we play strong; they open four-card majors, we open five; their two-bids are strong (Acol), ours are weak.

Directing an afternoon game, a British couple arrived to play, and the wife was wearing a housecoat and a shower cap over a full head of beer-can-sized hair curlers. A dentist from Texas took exception to her appearance and said something to her. Her husband took umbrage and made ready to defend his wife's honor. Their voices escalated and the Brit shoved the dentist. Instinctively, I rushed to the table and separated the men.

"That man," sputtered the Brit, "called my wife a disgrace."

"Did you?" I asked the American.

"I did, but just look at her. She is a disgrace."

I summoned my diplomacy. "Whether or not, 'a disgrace' is forcing for one round."

Later, I reported the incident to the Cruise Director. She grimaced, "This five-star ship is getting less five-star every day."

In the 1970's, I was staffing a cruise to Bermuda. I seem to recall that the ship was the *Sea Venture*; it docked in Hamilton on Monday morning and was scheduled to return to New York on Thursday afternoon. From my perspective, this was an ideal assignment. Bermuda was my favorite island to visit, and there were no duties while the ship was in port. Either Tuesday or Wednesday, I rode my motorbike out to Horseshoe Bay, brought a book and a blanket, and prepared to spend a sunny day on the beach. Around noon, lazily scanning the horizon, I saw a ship that looked remarkably similar to the *Sea Venture* sailing out to sea. It was disquieting, but I reassured myself that it wasn't Thursday and many cruise ships look alike, so I settled back with my book.

When I returned to Hamilton, my ship's berth was empty. I was about to panic when I noticed hundreds of people, some of whom I recognized as fellow passengers, lined up along the dock. What had happened was that the *Sea Venture* and other neighboring ships had responded to an S.O.S. from the *QE2*, which had lost power off Bermuda and was floating dead in the water. A hair-raising evacuation of the *QE2* passengers in rough seas was taking place, and our ship returned to Hamilton at the end of the day, filled with *QE2* people. Some were offloaded to Bermuda hotels, others stayed on board the *Sea Venture* and traveled back to New York with us. Space was tight but we managed. The *QE2* was much too large to be docked in Bermuda, so replacement engine parts were flown to her by helicopter. The *QE2* had a checkered history, including running aground off Martha's Vineyard. She was also converted into a troop ship during the Falkland Islands war.

*   *   *

My association with the Goren organization produced other benefits. For many years, the Goren books and column were ghost-written by a stable of bridge writers. In the mid 1970's, I was asked to ghost some columns. My mentor was Richard Frey, a fine player and Editor-in-Chief of the early editions of the ACBL's *Official Bridge Encyclopedia*. He patiently explained to me how to choose appropriate material that could be condensed to fit the limited space. Learning to write compactly stood me in good stead in later years when I was granted my own byline.

By 1980, I was included on the masthead of the Goren Editorial Board. I had ghosted a few of their books, including a revision of *Goren's Bridge Complete*, a massive tome first published in 1942. It saw many revisions but had lagged way behind current expert thinking. Outdated as it was, it was still a consistent best-seller because Goren remained a household name, long after he ceased playing and writing.

I've already explained my brief connection to the Goren television show, but I also had the chance to make a movie with Omar Sharif. No, it wasn't in the Arabian desert or deep in Russia. It was an instructional bridge video, *Play Bridge With Omar*

Sharif and Dorothy Hayden Truscott, and I was used as set dressing, but I did spend a whole day with Sharif on the "set." The circumstances: Tannah Hirsch, who had assumed Harold Ogust's role as the head of the Goren organization, chose the elegant Regency Whist Club in New York City as the site for taping, an appropriate setting for the movie star Sharif.

I was a member of the club with my first wife, Carroll, and we were chosen as being photogenic (at least she was) and sophisticated about bridge (we both were). Dorothy and Omar were the teachers, and after the lessons had been taped, the four of us sat and played a few deals in front of the cameras. This segment was eventually used as background while the credits rolled.

Sharif was as magnetic in person as on the screen. Those coal-black eyes seemed to burn with interest whenever a subject interested him, such as bridge or women. At this stage of his career, he was making movies to fund his bridge and gambling ventures. Years before, he headlined and played with the Omar Sharif Bridge Circus, a touring group of international stars. The Circus traveled to major cities to play challenge matches against a team of local experts. In 1975, Lancia automobiles became the sponsor of the Circus tour. If the local team won, each victor received a Lancia. Since the Circus included several of the Italian Blue Team stalwarts, Lancia assumed it wouldn't part with many cars. This were mistaken; in three of the four American cities on the tour, the local experts won. It was good publicity for Sharif and bridge, but it's doubtful that Lancia got its money's worth.

CHAPTER 5

BRIDGE AND MUSIC, A HARMONIOUS DUO

I've been fortunate to have had numerous mentions in *The New York Times*. One of my favorites, by Alan Truscott, appeared in early 1980 and could use some amplification. Leonard Pennario was an internationally-respected concert pianist who also loved bridge. He happened to be visiting New York City to renew a contract with Columbia Records, and he contacted the Truscotts, wondering if a bridge game might be available. Knowing my interest in classical piano, Alan got in touch, and we arranged to play as a foursome in a Long Island Swiss event: the Truscotts paired up, and the pianists formed a new partnership.

At the dinner break, Leonard wanted to discuss the deals to take advantage of the expert company, and I wanted him to discourse on classical music, taking advantage of his long and successful concert career. We compromised by talking about Cole Porter and Gilbert & Sullivan. Alan was a huge G & S fan and Pennario loved the witty, worldly Porter lyrics.

Pennario lived in Los Angeles at a time when Alfred Sheinwold had recently moved there. Sheinwold possessed a lyrical tenor (I had accompanied him when I was a lad) and was familiar with German lieder. Pennario contacted Sheinwold and suggested that they swap bridge lessons for music sessions—Alfie would sing, while Leonard would accompany, later they would play bridge together. I'm told that this arrangement lasted a long time, because each man thought he had the better of the bargain.

Back in New York, Alan Truscott penned a column for *The Times* on March 3, 1980. He noted that the worlds of music and bridge infrequently intersect, because each is so demanding of time. Nonetheless, on this rare occasion, two pianists found themselves in a duet, displaying a deft touch while successfully defending a doubled game contract.

South dealer
East-West vulnerable

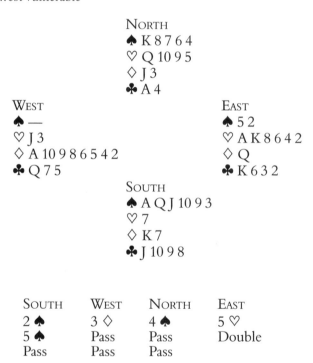

NORTH
♠ K 8 7 6 4
♡ Q 10 9 5
◇ J 3
♣ A 4

WEST
♠ —
♡ J 3
◇ A 10 9 8 6 5 4 2
♣ Q 7 5

EAST
♠ 5 2
♡ A K 8 6 4 2
◇ Q
♣ K 6 3 2

SOUTH
♠ A Q J 10 9 3
♡ 7
◇ K 7
♣ J 10 9 8

SOUTH	WEST	NORTH	EAST
2 ♠	3 ◇	4 ♠	5 ♡
5 ♠	Pass	Pass	Double
Pass	Pass	Pass	

South committed a cardinal sin in the auction when he bid five spades. A player who preempts has presumably told his complete story and should leave further decisions to partner. The problem was that South was too strong for a weak-two; his correct opening was one spade. Having initially underbid, he trapped himself into a later indiscretion. If he had passed, North would have happily doubled five hearts for a sizable penalty.

Against five spades doubled, West (Pennario) led the heart jack. If South had covered routinely with dummy's queen, East (me) would have been compelled to win. An easy shift to my singleton queen of diamonds would have produced a ruff for down two.

When South didn't cover with dummy's queen, I had a problem. Overtaking to shift to diamonds would work poorly if South held the diamond ace, because dummy's hearts could easily be established for discards.

Therefore, at trick one, I followed with the heart deuce, what Truscott termed "a technical pianissimo." When the jack of hearts held, Pennario realized that I must have the ace-king, yet I did not want a continuation. Cleverly, he shifted to the diamond ace and continued the suit, giving us plus 500 for down two.

My five-heart call was a rash bid but made for a sound reason. Average opponents usually assume an expert knows what he's doing. They believed my bid and sacrificed. This is one of the poker elements of bridge.

*   *   *

Playing bridge and performing music share some simple connections. Both require counting, concentration, and an ability to perform under pressure. Defending and bidding are similar to collaborating in chamber music, declaring is like playing a solo.

Bridge and music share a mathematical linkage. Both depend on recognizing patterns and sequence. In bridge, knowing hand patterns that add to thirteen, such as 4-4-3-2, 5-4-3-1, etc., will help your memory and counting. If you memorize your hand's distribution, or the dummy when it appears, it can help you recall what has been played. If you are declaring and trying to get a count on an opponent's distribution, familiarity with the combinations that add to thirteen is useful. In music, rock and roll has patterns and sequence. The harmony progresses from I-IV-V-I, meaning that if the piece starts in the key of C (I), the harmonic progression is C-F-G-C, and it keeps repeating that pattern. In classical music, many melodies are patterned. The famous opening phrase of Beethoven's Fifth Symphony descends a minor third (from G to E-Flat). The next phrase starts a full tone lower and uses the same minor third descent (F to D). That motif is repeated throughout the first movement. Rhythm is also patterned; in pop songs, it is highly repetitive, but so is a waltz or march. Recognizing micro-patterns helps analyze how a piece of music is put together, and it is also a memory aid to the performer.

On a more complex level, bridge and music exploit the use of limited space. In bridge, bidding space starts at one club and extends through seven notrump; in western music, the span is the twelve tones of the chromatic scale. The system builder or composer creates imaginative, pleasing, and effective structures within the imposed space limitations by ordering sequences.

In bridge, let's say you want to build a comprehensive system of responding to partner's one-notrump opening. You begin with the structures that a two-club response is Stayman, while two diamonds and two hearts are transfers into the adjacent major. This leaves two spades free to mean something other than spades. You decide to use it as a "two-under" transfer to three clubs: two spades is two steps below three clubs on the bidding ladder. For parallelism (pattern), you use two notrump as a transfer to three diamonds. The extra space of the "two-under" transfer can be utilized to allow opener to indicate whether he has a good fit for responder's minor. For example, after one notrump — two spades, opener can bid two notrump to say that he likes clubs, and three clubs to deny a good fit (or vice-versa).

So far, so good, but how does responder raise to two notrump with a balanced hand and 8–9 points if two notrump has been dedicated as a transfer to diamonds? The solution is a two-step approach: start with two clubs (Stayman), and after a two-diamond reply continue with two notrump, natural and invitational, neither promising nor denying a four-card major.

Responder has used the bidding space from two clubs to two notrump judiciously to describe useful holdings, leaving the entire three-level free for other meanings. Three clubs can show both minors, at least five-five, and invite game; three diamonds can show the same distribution but a stronger hand, 10-plus points and a game-force. Three hearts and three spades can be used in parallel fashion to show five-five hands with the majors, or one could use three-level bids as splinters, and there are other possibilities as well. The point is to construct a method that covers as many frequent hand-types as possible and still, when necessary, finish in three notrump, a playable contract. The key to a good structure is the efficient use of bidding space.

In music, structure defines how space is filled with the twelve chromatic pitches from the start of a piece to the middle to the finish. The sonata-allegro structure used by Beethoven (in early works), Haydn, Mozart, and other Classicists, begins with an opening theme in the tonic key and a contrasting theme in the dominant. Then, there is a development of both themes that moves through more-distant harmonic regions, a return to the tonic (home base), and a recapitulation of the two main themes (this time both in the tonic key). A brief coda may follow. Recognizing the themes and harmonic relationships allows the musician to comprehend how the music is put together on a "macro level," and this helps the performer communicate the sweep of a substantial piece, highlighting climaxes. The listener with musical background is able to follow the composer's road map and appreciate the music on a mental as well as an emotional level. The way themes and harmonies are sequenced provides grounding and direction, just as a high-low signal on defense or a fast-arrival bidding sequence are meaningful.

When does one become a professional-caliber bridge player or musician? The key is to start young, the earlier the better. Most professional instrumentalists took their first music lessons before they were of school age. (Singers tend to start later, after puberty when their voice has settled, although they may study music appreciation as youngsters.) Bridge experts have generally reached a high level by the time they are in their late teens. They are already sophisticated about card play and bidding theory. As they progress through their twenties, they learn to refine their judgment, which depends on acquiring additional experience.

Almost every student that I, or my colleagues, teach didn't begin serious bridge until later in life, women usually after their nest empties, men after retirement. Consequently, teacher and student must realistically confront the limitations imposed by life's timetable. Bridge can still become a great asset in many ways, but achieving expert status may no longer be in the cards.

How does a bridge player or musician become expert? The young bridge player needs to find a like-minded partner and play against the best competition available. When not playing, read and study how the experts think. The path to bridge expertise is enjoyable. The path to musical expertise is different: Find a good teacher, listen to the best musicians perform, and practice, practice, practice. The last part can be drudgery and often drives people away. To make muscle memory training endurable, if not enjoyable, is an important goal. I think the parallel is an athlete's training. Whether in the weight room, or on the driving range, the athlete must always be goal-oriented. The prize must be worth the pain or the potential boredom of endless repetitions.

Finally, bridge and music can be appreciated on both an emotional and a cerebral level. Brilliant coups are aesthetically and intellectually satisfying, whether executed by an individual or a partnership. And music is nourishment for body and soul. When I'm able to combine bridge and music in my writing or teaching, it's a special pleasure, as in this excerpt from *The Bridge World*, July 2004.

HITTING THE RIGHT NOTES
BY AUGUST W. BOEHM

Some things are too difficult for anyone beyond childhood to learn. Take piano playing. Suppose one wishes to study a moderately difficult Beethoven sonata, *The Tempest, Opus 31, No.2*. The first eight measures take only a few seconds to play, yet contained within are 73 notes, 13 phrasing marks, three tempo indications, three crucial pedal instructions, 16 notations of a specific kind of touch, nine marks that pertain to dynamics, 23 fingerings specified by an editor, two structurally significant pauses, and an embellishment that must be correctly interpreted. On top of all that, tone production and other artistic matters must be considered, all within just eight measures. That is not a large part of the piece; the first movement contains 226 measures, the second 103, the last 398.

The pianist is expected to grasp and control all these elements simultaneously and to make doing so second nature, to be free to concentrate on delivering an artistic, convincing performance. To achieve this complex multi-tasking, neural paths must be trained from an early age, the earlier the better, to link brain, fingers, and, if you will, soul. The goal is attained by hundreds of talented virtuosi and thousands of teachers from conservatories worldwide each year, but the most successful all started young, usually very young (pre-school age). Headline musical careers that began as child prodigies are commonplace.

What has this to do with bridge? For one thing, training an adult from beginner to top-flight tournament champion is virtually impossible. The best players are usually expert by the time they reach adulthood, many while in their teens. They receive their early stimuli while the brain is nimble enough to grasp the game's complexities, to recognize patterns and sequence, and to do everything quickly, freeing the mind to meet the game's greater challenges. Counting an opponent's hand and mastering complex systems are a young expert's points of departure. They still need to learn how to play with and against other masters, just as the serious pianist who conquers the notes and expression marks still must learn how to make music and captivate audiences. At this point, experience becomes the best teacher. Music and bridge contain much that cannot be formally taught, although some of that can be learned.

As a bridge teacher, you will probably never encounter a student with professional aspirations and talent. Instead, you will be the bridge equivalent of a music teacher assisting people searching for an enriching endeavor, who want to play commendably in front of friends. You mustn't sneer, either inwardly or otherwise, just because you are operating far from the lofty spires of your expertise. It isn't as glamorous as coaching the stars, but it is more important, because the stars can learn on their own.

Customizing instruction is key; you must be able to find problems that suit a current student's needs. If your bridge student requires a little Chopin or Schumann to breathe the Romantic era into a narrow education, try this: With neither side vulnerable, you open one heart holding:

♠ 10 3 ♡ A K 10 8 5 2 ♢ — ♣ A K Q 5 4

The playing strength is there for a two-club opening, but the concentrated high cards are apt to spell disappointing defense. Bidding two clubs invites experienced opponents to compete with shape, especially when not vulnerable, leaving you poorly placed should the bidding develop along the lines of: two clubs

— two spades — pass — four spades — ?, where you are yet to mention either of your suits.

You open one heart, partner raises to two hearts ("semi-constructive," as in Bridge World Standard, about 8-9 points with three-plus trumps). The opponents remain silent. What is your plan? Clearly, slam is possible; even a grand is not out of the question—ace-king of spades and four trumps, for example. However, even five hearts may be too high, with two spade losers and a heart loser. What approaches make sense?

A convention-oriented player might toy with five diamonds, Exclusion Blackwood (instructing partner to ignore the ace of diamonds in his key-card reply). This will uncover the ace of spades, but the slam-worthy king-queen of spades would remain below the radar, and the trump issue is not broached. What about an autosplinter of four diamonds? If partner signs off at four hearts, a five-of-a-minor continuation should demand that he reveal a spade control. That's an improvement, but do you want to reach slam any time partner has first- or second-round control of spades?

How about a slower approach? Bid three clubs, showing length, prepared to control-bid four diamonds and five diamonds later, again demanding that partner show spade control. This seems to be the best technical way to handle the problem, remaining low enough for partner to control-bid both four spades and five spades with the ideal spade holding. Opener could then produce a six-club grand-slam-try to focus on trump quality.

However, there is another way to go: the deceptive route. Six hearts might succeed missing the two top spades, if the opponents lead something else. Clubs could provide discards from dummy, or the diamond-ace lead may promote dummy's values in that suit. How might you induce these events?

One way is the musty stratagem of bidding two spades as a lead-inhibitor; another is to play it straight with three clubs but later control-bid in spades, hoping to induce a diamond lead. Or, one could psych a three-spade splinter or even a four-spade Exclusion Blackwood excursion to try to produce the desired effect. Might you vary your tactics depending on whether it was pairs or teams, especially if contemplating one of the deceptive routes? You surely might. If your operation fails, to how many people are you willing to apologize? And it would make sense to temper your strategy based on what you know about your left-hand opponent.

There are no concrete answers, but I like the problem, because it is apt to be useful to the technically-oriented student who has never glimpsed the tactical side of bridge; this infusion of the Romantic ought to expand possibilities. At high levels, a player without imagination is seriously handicapped. Even if he never steps out himself, he must know what his opponents might be doing. And if the student is all feeling and instinct but lacks technical knowledge of classical forms, the scientific alternatives in this problem may open new horizons.

*   *   *

A good ear is an asset for bridge and music. Experts of yore like Harry Fishbein and Al Roth, to name two that I knew, were known for uncanny "table-feel." They seemed to have a sixth sense that helped them place missing honors during the early play. On a clear day, their seeming clairvoyance gave opponents the creeps.

Meet Oswald Jacoby, another legend, whom I met in Texas when I visited John Bromberg during our collegiate summers. Ozzie was the youngest man to pass all the actuarial exams. He won championships over a span of seven decades and during 1962 replaced Goren as the top all-time masterpoint winner.

Ozzie was the most rapid-fire talker I ever heard, and he was capable of multitasking on a startling level. I saw him simultaneously play a game of lightning chess (ten seconds per move) while answering a bridge question and watching a sporting event on television, and he was in full command of all three. When he was given a bidding problem, especially one that involved a competitive sequence, he sometimes refused to answer. "I'd have to be there," he explained. He meant that his table-feel could supply a clue as to whether an opponent was light or held full values. He used to maintain that if he misguessed a two-way finesse for a queen, he had misplayed, not misguessed. He assumed he had overlooked some subtle indication. All these legends were intuitive thinkers; they might not be able to describe how they reached their conclusions, but their results were impressive.

A musician obviously benefits from a good ear, and I'm able to use my ear training to good effect at the bridge table. Before the advent of silent bidding with bidding boxes, players spoke their calls and often they revealed more than they should. A sulky pass, a resonant double, or a wavering two-club overcall spoke volumes. There is nothing illegal in using information gleaned from an opponent; the trouble comes when a player uses partner's intonation to advantage. This opens the chasm to unauthorized information, the bane of tournament bridge.

Bidding boxes have been helpful in reducing the inferences that arise from vocal inflections, but there is still the issue of tempo. Unduly slow or fast actions can create unauthorized information. Seasoned players know this and try to regulate their tempo, especially against experts with good ears. A musician is accustomed to feeling a meter, a regular pulse. When the tempo changes, even slightly, the pulse changes. If my opponent's normal tempo is two to four seconds before acting, and he takes six, it registers. His action wasn't obvious, and I start thinking about what might have caused his problem. Was he slightly off-shape;

was he heavy for his bid, or was he light? There isn't always an answer, but it starts the engines.

The acid test comes when a player must decide between an orthodox action and an anti-percentage bid or play based on table-feel. Many experts always take the percentage action. They don't want to look bad or open themselves to criticism from their peers. Others, myself included, have enough confidence to back their table judgment and choose an action based on feel, regardless of percentages. Here's a recent example:

NORTH
♠ 7 6 4
♡ Q 8 5 2
◇ K 7 6
♣ Q J 8

SOUTH
♠ A Q 5
♡ 7 6 3
◇ A J 9 4
♣ A K 5

East dealt and passed; sitting South I opened one diamond; West passed; partner responded one heart. East passed, I rebid two notrump and partner raised to three notrump. At this point, East flickered before passing. A flicker is a slight break from that player's normal tempo. What could the reason be? East must have briefly considered doubling three notrump; it is unimaginable to pass twice and then bid over three notrump.

Such a double would be Lightner, a lead-director. Here, it calls for the lead of dummy's first-bid suit, hearts. File this information away. West leads a low spade, East produces the king, and we win the ace. By the way, if West noticed his partner's flicker, he is bound to disregard it as unauthorized information. A heart lead would be highly unethical.

To make the contract, we need four diamond tricks. That requires a lucky lie of the missing diamonds. If East was dealt queen-third and West three low, the normal procedure, low to the king and finesse the jack, will win the needed four tricks.

Reconcile this possibility with East's flicker. East is a favorite to hold long hearts headed by the ace-king, maybe with the jack—remember, he almost doubled three notrump for a heart lead. If he had been dealt the diamond queen, along with the known spade king and the presumed heart ace-king-plus-length, he would have opened the bidding. Therefore, place the diamond queen with West.

To score four diamond tricks, a backward finesse is indicated. Lead the jack and plan to let it ride. If the jack is covered, win dummy's king and finesse your nine. The backward finesse is anti-percentage, because it requires two cards in favorable position, the diamond queen with West and the diamond ten with East. The straightforward finesse requires only the diamond queen with East. Despite this, table-feel indicated it was my best chance, and I was willing to look foolish if my inferences were incorrect. The full deal:

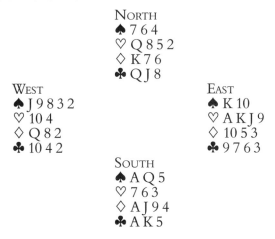

NORTH
♠ 7 6 4
♡ Q 8 5 2
♢ K 7 6
♣ Q J 8

WEST
♠ J 9 8 3 2
♡ 10 4
♢ Q 8 2
♣ 10 4 2

EAST
♠ K 10
♡ A K J 9
♢ 10 5 3
♣ 9 7 6 3

SOUTH
♠ A Q 5
♡ 7 6 3
♢ A J 9 4
♣ A K 5

The diamonds came home, so all was well.

CHAPTER 6

THE CARRIAGE TRADE
TO SING-SING

The Card School was unique. Located in midtown New York City on Park Avenue, it was solely dedicated to teaching bridge. No duplicates, only supervised play to provide practice for students. The original faculty roster read like a *Who's Who* of bridge. The Card School published a booklet, *The Biggest Little Bridge Book in the World*, and it became a best-seller. In the 1960's, the school negotiated a deal with a major cigarette manufacturer. During that period, each pack of cigarettes had a coupon on the back, redeemable for one bridge booklet from the school.

The booklet was designed to offer concise advice to frequently asked questions. The Card School's clientele was strictly carriage trade. Steep prices, famous instructors, and a quiet, luxurious setting in the Beekman Hotel distinguished it from an ordinary duplicate bridge club.

In the mid 1970's, I was asked to join the faculty on a temporary basis—an instructor was quite ill, and it was intended that I substitute until he recovered. As fate decreed, he didn't recover, and my appointment became permanent. At the time, I was involved in music and theater projects in and around New York City. I had extra time and welcomed the additional income. In New York, it is common to discover that your attractive waitress or waiter is an out-of-work actor. "Out-of-work" is not the preferred term; "between jobs" sounds better. When I was between jobs, I found I could fall back on teaching bridge for income.

The Card School was considered an authority in the teaching field. As the newest staff member, I often arrived early and cleared the answering machine of phone messages. Sometimes, the caller had a question about the right bid or play on a deal from the night before. Questions came from as far away as Johannesburg, South Africa.

I used the school's syllabus when teaching; it dovetailed with the booklet's advice. Occasionally, I audited a class taught by one of my distinguished colleagues. Boris Koytchou, a polished gentleman and excellent speaker, was delivering a lecture about trump management, basically about when to draw trumps. At the conclusion of the lecture, before the students were to play prepared deals, he asked if there were any questions. Diffidently, a person in the back raised her hand.

"Mr. Koytchou, some of us at our table were wondering, just what is a trump?"

Jim Becker and Edgar Kaplan had recently left the faculty, and the day-to-day management was left to Larry Markes and me, both of us in our early thirties. The school continued to prosper, and I gained a lot of experience teaching. As I look back, I realize that my presentations have become much more compact. Previously, I allowed all sorts of digressions and qualifications to creep in. There is a natural tendency to succumb to this flaw, because an instructor knows so much more than his students. Unconsciously, perhaps, he wishes the students to acknowledge his expertise, and he adds too much extraneous information. A better approach is to offer advice in easily digestible bites, and repeat, repeat, repeat.

To an instructor from the distinguished Card School, other teaching avenues automatically opened. At a large social club (distinct from a bridge club) where I was already established as a duplicate director, I was approached to conduct a series of classes. During the summer, country clubs in Long Island called the Card School to request an instructor. Word-of-mouth is important in this narrow band of the bridge world, and I found my business expanding. Once in a while, someone would hire me to play a duplicate session, or a social club would seek a duplicate director. Meanwhile, the cruise opportunities remained intact.

Within a few years, the Card School suffered a mortal blow when its lease expired, and the hotel demanded a huge increase in rent. Negotiations were futile, and we sought comparable space in a suitable location. Alas, the rentals were similarly high—the Card School had been operating under a long-term, sweetheart lease, and now the bubble had burst.

Larry Markes decided to move to California, and I reluctantly abandoned the project. Minus our famous instructors, business had fallen off slightly, and other bridge clubs in Manhattan were offering capable instruction at lower rates. Woody Allen took over our space for use in his movie business. An era ended, but my bridge career was launched.

At this point in my life, I accepted any and all jobs. For example, I volunteered to teach a class at Sing-Sing, the penitentiary in Ossining, New York. I was approached by a delegate of the ABA, the American Bridge Association, which represented African-Americans, a holdover from the days when parts of the ACBL were all white. The delegate wanted someone to instruct inmates scheduled for imminent release. The idea was to ease their reintroduction to society. I'm not sure how bridge fit in; perhaps because it was considered a socializing activity, it qualified. The drive up the Hudson was scenic, and we arrived at a forbidding structure with masses of barbed wire and guard posts. We were screened for weapons. The guards wore none, the fear being that guns could be turned against them. This was the minimum-security zone—up the hill in maximum-security, I'm told, matters were very different.

I was shown to a cinder-block meeting room, given a board and chalk, and about a dozen inmates were escorted into the area. I found it a truculent audience and was hard-pressed to engage them. Thinking it might be amusing, I began a discussion of the hold-up play, but my sponsor shook his head and I switched topics. I wonder if any of the inmates eventually found their way to "The Bucket of Blood."

This was my second encounter with prisoners. The first had occurred years earlier when I was playing high-stakes money bridge at the Mayfair Club in New York. It was during a summer when I was teaching school, and, with time on my hands, I decided to send myself to bridge "finishing school." The best way to hone one's game is to play against people better than you for stakes you can't quite afford. The idea is to put yourself under pressure and learn how to handle it. As a recitalist, I was already accustomed to performing under pressure. It's not an easy thing to handle, and practice helps.

The Mayfair was a rough-and-tumble public bridge club. At the time, it featured teams-of-four scored at imps. The teams were determined by lot. Each player was assigned a number, similar to golf handicaps. The scratch players were zero, the next best were one, all the way up to six for the weakest. A captain was selected at random, and the captain drew lots for his three teammates. The handicaps for the team were totaled and converted into imps. A team with a zero, a two, a three, and a five had a total of 10 imps. This was compared to the other team's total and determined the handicap. Three-way matches were handicapped the same way. At the end of the short match, the imp handicap was added or subtracted from the final result. When I played, the stake was $2.00 per imp, with a bonus for winning the match. A few hundred dollars could easily change hands in an evening, heady stakes for someone on a school teacher's salary in the early 1970's.

Over the summer, I had my ups and downs, but eventually I won money and toughened my game. The other players included some of the world's best, like Al Roth and Ira Rubin, the latter aptly nicknamed The Beast for the way he treated partners. The next generation of experts like Alan Sontag and Peter Weichsel were well-represented, plus an assortment of characters who cared nothing about masterpoints but understood bridge.

Two of the characters I'll call Rodney and Tito. Rodney was a young near-expert, much impressed with his own game. Tito was an older man, fairly solid, but in that company one of the weaker players. One evening, Rodney found himself partnered with Tito. In Rodney's eyes, Tito could do nothing right. Every bid or play drew increasingly abusive criticism, extreme even for that group. Tito started to lose patience. In a thick Italian accent, he told Rodney, "Shut up, I've heard enough."

This only incited Rodney to new heights of sarcasm. Finally, Tito put his cards face down on the table and muttered, "I gotta make a phone call." He pushed himself up from the table and went to the elevator. Someone pulled Rodney aside.

"Do you know who Tito is?"

"A rotten bridge player."

"Ask Roth."

Rodney scorned advice, but he respected Al Roth, as did everyone who called himself a bridge player. Rodney asked Roth, "Who is this Tito jerk?"

"Tito used to have his bridge magazines forwarded to him in Sing-Sing. If you got him mad, you should leave. Now."

Rodney turned white and rushed for the elevators. On his way down, the up elevator was carrying a guy named Sheldon, who played at the Mayfair. Sheldon never removed his jacket, and it wasn't because the Mayfair had a dress code. Hardly. It was the tools of his trade he carried underneath.

Tito returned with Sheldon in tow. "Where's the punk?"

It turned out that the punk was headed for a plane to the West coast. For months, Rodney phoned the Mayfair, asking if was safe to return. Ironically, both Sheldon and Tito were known to be highly ethical at the bridge table, even though considerable money was involved. Breaking the rules of bridge was not part of their code.

*   *   *

Lady Luck can operate in amusing ways. Back in New York in the late 1970's, I received a call from a prominent social club, requesting a duplicate director. I accepted and arrived to fulfill my obligation. The event involved three different clubs, each with multiple teams. The idea was to run an event where the winning club could be determined, as well as the top pairs. This movement is tricky, and I wasn't adequately prepared.

In the middle of the session, one pair complained that they had already played the boards on their table. I exchanged their boards with another table. A round later, two pairs made the same complaint, and a third table said they had previously played their current opponents. From there, it got worse.

By the end of the session, I had removed some boards from play, introduced others, given two pairs a bye round, and left everyone with the feeling that the tournament was in shambles. I fudged some scores, declared winners, collected my check, and departed. "Never hear from them again," I thought. "Serves me right." I resolved to be more careful in the future.

A year later, I got a call from the same club. It was a different chairperson. "We were given your name and were told that you conduct duplicates." Gingerly, I acknowledged same.

"We'd like you to run our annual three-way club champion-ship." I agreed.

"Very good. I'm sure you'll be better than the fellow last year who made a real mess of it."

For decades since, this club has become my chief provider of lessons. Ironic, isn't it? After I was safely installed as their direc-tor, a new head of the Card Committee approached me after a duplicate. "Young man," she intoned sternly. "Today, I held very poor cards, hardly an opening bid. See that it doesn't happen again."

It took some explaining.

CHAPTER 7

CHEATING: SCANDALS AND REACTIONS

In the Culbertson era, bridge had high visibility. Big matches made front-page news. Today, it takes a cheating scandal to move bridge off an inside page. Considering how easy it is to cheat at bridge, it's surprising that scandals have been so few.

Cheating takes many forms, from what used to be called "coffee-housing" to prearranged signaling. At the social level, players unwittingly pass extra information all the time through table talk, body language, facial mannerisms, and vocal inflections. In the purely social milieu, usually no one cares; they are at the table to have fun, enjoy each other's company, and play a few deals.

In duplicate, more formality is required. Table talk is forbidden, and players are expected to refrain from transmitting extraneous information. Bidding boxes make the auction silent, and, in the highest-level tournaments, screens are used. The screen is a thin diagonal wall, high enough to prevent a player from seeing his partner. North can see West, South sees East, and that's all. A cutout in the bottom of the screen allows the players to view the dummy and the cards played. Bidding is silent, the bidding cards are placed on a tray which is passed under the screen from one side of the table to the other. At first, it is a bit cumbersome, but experts who play under such conditions like it.

Screens came into use in the United States in 1974; in 1975, they were first used in international competition. In the beginning, screens were controversial. Some felt it gave the impression that cheating was rampant. However, the majority thought that screens would prevent accusations of cheating, as you can neither see nor hear your partner. What provoked their use?

As early as 1958 in Lake Como, an American star, the redoubtable Tobias Stone, made the front page by accusing the Italian Blue Team of cheating. His team had been beaten by Italy in the Bermuda Bowl, and Stoney was censured for making unproven accusations, but it wouldn't be the last time someone accused the Blue Team players. Not surprisingly, they indignantly denied the charges.

Experts with great table presence may pick up vibes that tell them something is wrong. They may not be able to pinpoint their suspicions, but the opponents' rhythm is off-kilter; they huddle at unexpected junctures. When the suspects swing for the fences, making a surprise lead or unlikely bid, they always hit a home run, they never strike out. It's the equivalent of a jury knowing in their bones that an accused is guilty, but it can't quite be proved. In such circumstances, the accused goes free, but, in the bridge world, suspicion and rumor follow the suspects.

The "elevator" method was employed by some cheats. The idea is to signal partner whether you hold a good hand for your previous bidding, fair values, or a poor hand. This type of information is especially helpful when the opponents preempt. Let's say that LHO opens two hearts with neither side vulnerable, partner and RHO pass. You hold:

♠ A J 8 ♡ 8 7 ◇ K Q 8 6 2 ♣ 9 5 2

Your options are double, three diamonds, and pass. All are fraught with peril; it depends on what you catch in partner's hand. If partner's hand is as good or better than yours, you could easily make a partscore, and the opponents might make two hearts. However, if partner has borscht, pass will be best.

Now, suppose partner held his cards high, at eye level, to indicate a good hand in context, around a minimum opening bid. It is safe to act. If partner holds his cards at chin level, he is showing about 7-10 points, and it will often pay to balance. Your pair may find a worthwhile sacrifice or push the opponents beyond their depth. If partner's cards are held low at chest level, he is showing less than seven points. Where the honest player must make his best guess, the cheat will find a bid when his side belongs in the auction and pass to avoid trouble when partner is weak. This is a sinister type of cheating, because it depends on prearranged signals. Sending illegal information about your range from maximum—middle range—minimum is especially useful to experts, whose seasoned judgment allows them to make good use of the information.

The use of screens put the elevator operators out of business.

In 1965, in Buenos Aires, two British stars, Terence Reese and Boris Shapiro, were accused by Americans of using finger signals to communicate the number of hearts each held. The accusations had become more precise, and the World Bridge Federation (WBF) reviewed the evidence, which included photographs of the accused varying their grips on their cards during play, sometimes held in awkward positions. Overwhelmingly, the WBF found the British pair guilty, and the British captain conceded his team's remaining matches. The matter was referred to the British Bridge League (BBL) for further disposition, but, after a ten-month inquiry, their verdict was "unproven." The WBF refused to accept the BBL's verdict, and Reese-Shapiro were not permitted to play in Bermuda Bowl contests until a three-year suspension had been satisfied.

The prevailing wisdom is that Shapiro was not on Reese's expert level. Reese, among the world's best players, was probably in the top five, Shapiro perhaps in the top thousand. An indication of possible cheating is that at least one member of the suspect pair is weaker than the competition they have consistently been defeating. If they decide to cheat, it's because they don't think they can win by playing it straight.

Screens were first used in the Bermuda Bowl competition of 1975, although some players found them demeaning. It was a bitter irony for bridge that this event was marred by the "foot-tapping" scandal. Two Italian players, Facchini and Zucchelli, were accused of touching each other's feet under the table, particularly before one had to make an opening lead. Coffee tables were placed under the card table to prevent further occurrences, but bad blood had been drawn, and the Americans refused to play against the accused Italian pair, unless ordered by the ACBL. Facchini and Zucchelli were eventually benched by their captain, and the Italians staged a furious rally to defeat the Americans. The WBF found the accused pair guilty of "improper conduct," and they were unwelcome in future international competitions.

In cheating accusations, there are basically two kinds of evidence: eyewitnesses and internal evidence. Eyewitness testimony often conflicts or is inconclusive, and when this is the case, the internal evidence is ultimately considered compelling. If the accused are cheating, it will be revealed by an examination of the deals. For instance, if the accused pair consistently takes anti-percentage actions that are successful, the premise is that they are using illegal signals. It takes an expert, sometimes a panel of experts, to evaluate the evidence of the deals. After the Buenos Aires affair, Reese and Alan Truscott each wrote a book that included a lengthy examination of many deals from that tournament. Reese exonerated himself, claiming that if he and his partner had knowledge of the heart suit, they would have achieved better results. Truscott, in contrast, found corroborating evidence of cheating in the deals. And the photographic evidence seemed damning.

Reese left behind a document, to be opened upon his death, in which he confessed that he and Shapiro had indeed used hand signals but had made no use of the information. Reese's purpose was to show how easy it was to transmit signals, even in international competition. Like all self-serving statements, the confession seems suspect. It's a shame that the episode left a permanent blot on his reputation, because Reese was undoubtedly one of the best bridge writers ever to grace the scene.

Let me create some examples to illustrate the evaluation of internal evidence. Suppose West holds:

♠ J 7 2 ♡ A 8 7 3 ◇ J 10 8 2 ♣ 10 4

South (RHO) opens one spade, North (LHO) responds three spades (an invitational raise), and South concludes the auction with four spades. Rate West's opening leads.

First choice is the diamond jack, top of an honor sequence in an unbid suit. Second choice, the club ten, top of an unbid doubleton. Third choice, a low trump. Many players would invert choices two and three. Fourth choice, the heart ace; laying down an ace without the king or shortness is usually a very poor lead.

Now, suppose West, from out of the blue, leads the heart three. Only a beginner would make such a lead—or a cheat! The lead of the heart three happens to catch East with king-deuce. East wins with the king, returns the deuce, and receives a heart ruff on the third round. This is the only defense to defeat the contract.

An expert would find this lead extremely suspicious. The heart three, virtually unthinkable, worked like a charm. It is too much of a coincidence. The conclusion is that West likely had knowledge of partner's heart holding, and that such knowledge could have been derived only illegally, not from bridge logic.

Try a bidding illustration. East holds:

♠ Q J 7 4 ♡ K 9 6 2 ◇ Q 8 3 ♣ 5 2

Playing five-card majors, West deals and opens one club, North (RHO) passes. The normal response is one heart, four-card majors up-the-line. Instead, East chooses to respond one notrump. This risks missing an eight-card fit in either major, leading to an inferior contract. However, it develops that West doesn't hold a four-card major, so notrump is indeed the best spot. Furthermore, the defenders are fooled into thinking that declarer lacks a four-card major, and their defense is apt to suffer.

Is this simply a case of East's making a lucky choice, the wrong bid at the right time? Possibly, but a pattern of such "lucky choices" will arouse suspicion.

I have created one extreme example, the opening lead of the heart three, and a more subtle one, the response of one notrump. A pair of expert cheats would not make the dramatic underlead of the heart three, even with illicit knowledge of partner's hand, because it raises a red flag. It's too weird with too great a payoff. West should grit his teeth and lead a normal diamond jack, realizing that the lead of the heart three exceeds the parameters of tolerance. If the cheats take advantage of every situation within their grasp, they quickly create suspicion. Better to use their signals when their actions are within the tolerance zone, that is, when another player at their skill level might make the same choice.

In the bidding example, is the one-notrump response within tolerance? Doubtful, but if the cheats are behind in the match and are trying to create a swing (that is, bid something reasonable but different from what is bid at the other table), then one notrump might meet the tolerance requirement. These are typical factors that expert judges must consider.

One might think that the introduction of screens would have eliminated charges of cheating, but in 1977 another scandal reared its ugly head. The United States Trial to determine its Bermuda Bowl team was abruptly aborted near the end of the final match when two members of one team, Richard Katz and Larry Cohen (not the Larry Cohen who writes in the monthly ACBL magazine) withdrew. This left their team with only three members, forcing that team to forfeit its final match when it had a comfortable lead. In addition, Cohen and Katz resigned from the ACBL.

What could have prompted such an outcome? It has been alleged that there were rumors of improper communication. A layman might well ask why a pair would resign on the verge of victory in a most prestigious event. Speculation ran rampant.

Formal charges hadn't been lodged; that was apparently part of the backroom deal—silence on the accuser's part in exchange for withdrawal. However, an accuser leaked information to the press, and this prompted Cohen and Katz to file suit against the ACBL and specific individuals for forty-four million dollars, essentially claiming defamation of character. After five years in the courts, the suit was dropped and Cohen and Katz were reinstated in the ACBL but not permitted to play as partners.

Disputes about cheating are notoriously difficult to prosecute in court. The judge and jury will be laymen, and internal evidence that might prove guilt to a bridge expert is apt to fall on untutored ears in a courtroom. To develop a solid case, short of a confession, the prosecutors must break the cheaters' code, present their findings to other players in private, and ask them to observe the accused to see if the predicted behavior is repeated.

For instance, suppose you think my partner and I are cheating because we have had too many results where our outlandish bids and plays prove successful. This internal evidence arouses your suspicion, as it should, but how do you make an airtight case?

It is necessary for you and your colleagues to observe us and discover our code. Let's say our opening leads have been uncanny over the course of many deals, perhaps months or even years. You should closely monitor opening leader's partner, who must be sending a helpful signal.

You notice that when we make an entry on our convention card after the auction is over, a perfectly normal practice, the pencil is replaced on the table in different positions. After lengthy observations, you conclude that when the pencil tip is pointing at partner, a spade is led, usually to our benefit. You pass this observation to a confederate and ask him to note the pencil positions. If your confederate comes to the same conclusion that whenever the pencil tip is pointing at opening leader, a spade opening lead is predictable, you have eyewitness testimony that a lay court can comprehend. Later, a bridge expert can analyze the deals and demonstrate why a spade lead was beneficial.

This is somewhat similar to the process that, in 1979, brought down Alan Cokin and Steve Sion, a prominent pair in national competitions. They were found guilty of using prearranged improper communication and expelled from the ACBL for five years. When Cokin and Sion reapplied for membership, it was granted with the proviso that they not play as a partnership. Since then, according to the current *Official Encyclopedia of Bridge*, Cokin "has devoted himself to overcoming this blemish on his record." Sion became involved in another violation of proprieties and was expelled permanently in 1997.

*   *   *

Let me demonstrate how easy it is to cheat: You and a fellow pro are playing in the same event, each with a client. If either of you wins some masterpoints for your client, there is a financial bonus, and the two pros believe in sharing the bonuses. You and your friend arrange to sit East-West in the same section. Both of you are familiar with the movement, so that when your friend stretches his arms, as a pre-arranged signal, you know that there is an easy-to-make slam in the cards. If it is early in a two-board round, the slam is on the first board; if late, the second board. The signal comes early in the round, and, knowing the movement, you calculate that your confederate is playing Boards 13 and 14. When you later encounter Board 13, if you hold a big hand or partner bids strongly, you intend to drive to slam. On Board 13, you hold:

♠ A Q 8 7 3   ♡ Q J 4   ◇ K Q 6 2   ♣ 6

You open one spade and partner raises to two spades, opponents silent. How can this be a slam, you wonder? Even four spades is far from certain. If you head to six spades, is this a credible action? Or does it exceed the range of tolerance? Clearly, the latter—no player of your caliber would commit to slam.

If you are disciplined (and very few cheats are), swallow hard, make a game-try, and, when partner accepts, settle for game.

Partner tables:

♠ 7 5 4 2   ♡ A 10 7   ◇ J 7 3   ♣ A 9 5

The heart king and club king are onside, and the trumps split two-two, so 12 tricks roll home. Don't be upset with your average score on this board; try to win the tournament on some other deal. If you bid the ridiculously lucky slam (about 10 percent) on an auction that makes no sense, tongues begin to wag. Cheats can't afford to appear suspicious.

A different scenario for the same board: Your partner passes, RHO passes, and this time you hold a weak hand. The slam must belong to your opponents, so should you bid in third seat with:

♠ 9 8 7 5 4 2 ♡ 6 ◇ J 10 3 ♣ 9 8 4

How about a spade preempt? If your side is not vulnerable and the opponents are, this is not an extreme action. In the modern game, a lot of players would open two spades, even three spades, in third seat at favorable vulnerability. If you do the same, you are operating within the bounds of tolerance.

However, suppose you decide to psych one heart or one no-trump. This is beyond the pale, and if it talks your opponents out of their laydown slam, as is probable, eyebrows are going to be raised. How coincidental for you to psyche and impede the opponents, just when they were dealt a slam.

Cheats tend to get greedy, which is how they get caught. They desperately need to win, which is usually why they turn to cheating. If both cheats were highly expert and content to use their illegal information only occasionally, without arousing suspicion, they could probably keep their illicit game going forever. Even their declarer play should benefit. If you know that you are likely to win the tournament because of your signals and your skill, it takes some of the pressure off. An unlucky result won't be crushing, because you know that you have good results in store.

Fortunately for the rest of us, the cheats are seldom content.

*   *   *

An ongoing problem for tournament organizers is the issue of deliberate dumping (intentionally losing part of an event) in order to improve one's overall chance of winning. This problem is hardly restricted to bridge—many other sports, and even the Olympics, have been plagued. In 2012, several women badminton competitors were suspended by the World Federation of Badminton for dumping matches in the qualifying rounds. The badminton players were trying to position themselves to advantage in the later brackets—they were losing early, hoping to win a medal. Is this wrong? Evidently, the Olympic Committee thought so.

In bridge, there is ongoing debate. Some feel that it is unsportsmanlike if a competitor does not try his hardest at all times. Others feel that there is nothing wrong with dumping a match if it helps you win the tournament. The fault lies with the organizers for placing the competitors in a compromised position.

In a knockout format, where the winner advances and the loser is eliminated, there is always incentive to win. However, let's say you are entered in a round-robin of sixteen teams, and the top four qualify for playoffs to determine the champion. You play each team once in the round-robin, and, before the final match, your team's cumulative score is high enough that your qualification is secure. In this final match, you are playing a relatively weak team on the cusp of qualifying. If you lose to them, they will make the playoffs, making it easier for your team in the final stage. If you beat them, they are out and you will face tougher competition. Should you play to win, or is it permissible to dump?

My feeling, widely shared in the expert bridge community, is that dumping in this situation is sportsmanlike, and the problem stems from negligent organizers who fail to create proper conditions of contest. It should never be to one's advantage to lose. If the organizer imposes a conflict of interest on the player, the organizer deserves the censure, not the player.

Bridge organizations in the United States have spent time and effort to create the best possible conditions of contest. Olympic committees have fallen short. In 2006, in a world pair event, a Chinese pair was in strong contention going into the final rounds. They played two other Chinese pairs who were faring poorly. The winning pair received four tops from the non-contending Chinese and vaulted into the winner's circle. Observers familiar with the deals are suspicious that there may have been deliberate dumping.

If so, do you blame the dumpers, who were motivated by national pride? Or should the blame, and there surely is blame, be assigned to the organizers, who failed to arrange the movement properly? Compatriots should play each other at the beginning of the session, when everyone is in contention, rather than at the end, when temptation may arise.

It's all very well to maintain that competitors must resist temptation and try their best at all times, but how do you enforce such a stricture? If a team loses a non-critical match, did it dump or simply play below par? Even top players have off days. Unless the dumping is egregious, how can an organization confidently censure competitors for losing, in what may have been an honest effort? Was it convenient for them to lose, or were they outplayed?

Hypothetically, say a team has already qualified for the playoff and faces a final round-robin match that is meaningless for both sides. The qualifying team is composed of three pairs; A and B are top-notch, C is notably weaker. If the team decides to rest pairs A or B, who have been playing daily for two weeks, and plays C throughout, does that constitute giving one's best effort? Not for the meaningless match, but surely it is sensible preparation for the playoffs. Should these players be condemned?

What about a team captain confronted by this dilemma? If he puts forward his best lineup for the meaningless match, his team (or countrymen, if it's an international event) may well blame him for short-sightedness, concerning himself with nickels and dimes when he should be focused on winning the gold medal. If, instead, he rests his stars, he will be blamed in some quarters for unsportsmanlike conduct. Whatever he does, he is subject to criticism, and this is an evil arrangement.

Furthermore, if the organizers decide to censure or ban competitors for unsportsmanlike conduct, there is the threat of a lawsuit. It seems far better to avoid such conundrums by providing incentives to win at every stage of the tournament.

*   *   *

Dumping is not funny, but almost everything in life has a humorous side. You may remember how our Columbia team dumped some imps against Dartmouth to avoid being stranded in wintry Keene, New Hampshire. This next story is based on reliable information. A successful, established team-of-four is badgered by a newcomer to the community who wants to be added to the team, if only as a roving substitute. This Fifth is a strong player but with an unfortunate, abrasive personality, and he won't take evasive responses or an outright "No" for an answer. Finally, three members of the team hatch a plot.

They will invite Mr. Fifth to join them in a pivot rubber bridge game for significant stakes and make it clear that this is his audition. To ensure that he finishes the big loser, flunking the test, the threesome decides to dump whenever he is their partner. Since Mr. Fifth is a pretty sophisticated player, the dumping must be artful, lest it arouse suspicion.

Early in the evening, the invitee is enjoying good cards, and he is winning. This needs to be rectified. On the next deal, Mr. Fifth picks up a balanced 19 HCP. He opens one club, his partner responds one diamond, and he rebids two notrump. Responder now has a problem because he is looking at a balanced 16 HCP. If he makes the normal bid, six notrump, the contract will likely succeed, and Mr. Fifth will surge further ahead. If he makes the outrageous underbid of three notrump, it will look like dumping. A raise to four notrump is possible, but if Mr. Fifth accepts the invitation and jumps to six notrump, the contract will be a favorite to make, and the operation will have failed.

Responder produces a clever solution. He jumps to seven notrump. If eyebrows are raised when he tables his dummy, he will admit to stretching his values, trying to recover early losses. The opening lead is made, Mr. Fifth breaks a side suit three-three, wins a finesse, and scores up his 15-percent grand slam. His margin mounts.

In the final rubber, one of the team desperately opens five clubs holding ace-king-queen-fifth of clubs and out. When Mr. Fifth questions the wisdom of such a bid, opener lamely replies, "I opened five clubs because I had five clubs." It had come to that.

At the end of the evening, Mr. Fifth is the big winner, the only player plus on the ledger. As he pockets the cash, he is probably thinking to himself, "That fourth member of the team who wasn't here tonight—he must be the greatest player on the planet to win with these three bozos."

Ironically, the dumping session did produce one desired outcome. Mr. Fifth never asked to be included again. These guys were obviously hopeless.

*   *   *

You might have gained the impression that bridge is a bottomless cesspool of deplorable behavior, but, in fact, conduct and ethics today are vastly improved from when I started to play. The ACBL deserves credit for educating its players about expected standards of behavior. A zero-tolerance policy for bad actors was instituted and has been adhered to. Specifically, rudeness to partner and opponents is no longer tolerated. What most often drives newcomers away from duplicate are boorish players, and the ACBL is in the business of recruiting and retaining new members. Efforts to increase membership have been successful, no doubt linked to less-offensive conduct.

The ethical standard is also vastly improved from when I started playing. To illustrate, if partner opened one club, an opponent preempted three spades, and you held a borderline bid which required you to stop and think, your partner often indicated whether he welcomed you into the auction. If he remained intensely interested in the proceedings, his one-club opening contained extra values. If he folded up his cards or started looking around the room, affecting disinterest, he held a balanced minimum. Some players at lower levels play like that today, but better players and tournament organizations explicitly disapprove.

In the old days, a well-known professional shamelessly instructed students on how to inflect their penalty doubles. A crisp, fast double was never to be taken out; the doubler had his opponents nailed. A slower double was less emphatic; partner could pull if in doubt, and a truly agonized double underlined the doubler's serious doubt. Partner was expected to react accordingly. And this expert was not alone. Far from it; a significant percentage of experts believed that this was how bridge should be played. If you acted without thought when you had a borderline decision, that was the equivalent of partner-baiting. You're supposed to help partner out. How could you expect to win?

A quixotic West Coast expert was said to have invested a significant amount of his own funds, testing a theory at the rubber bridge table. He believed that obvious defensive leads are made much more rapidly than speculative leads. Singletons are led faster than doubletons. On defense against suit contracts, when he had a singleton, an A-list lead, he paused significantly before leading it. Doubletons, on the B- or C-list, he led at the speed of light. His partners were constantly blowing tricks, failing to give him ruffs when he was void, chasing phantom ruffs when he led from doubletons. The expert was deliberately making it hard on partner; how could he expect to win? He didn't, but he proved his point—many players are more influenced by the *manner* in which a card is played than by the card itself.

A player's natural tendency is to make easy bids and plays quickly, while less-obvious moves require thought. Still, an uneven tempo creates clear implications, and players of an older generation felt free to capitalize. There is a moral for today's player; when you are declarer, use your musician's ear and pay attention to the tempo of the opening lead. It often provides a clue to the play. There is nothing unethical about using "table presence" clues *provided by opponents*; it is a skill and an asset.

One of the pioneers in cleaning up the ethical arena was the late Edgar Kaplan, long-time Editor of *The Bridge World* magazine. Edgar wrote a seminal article that referred to "Old Black Magic," what older players, schooled in the loose ethics of their youth, regularly employed. Apart from carefully calibrated penalty doubles, bidding systems used to be much less sophisticated, filled with many gaping systemic gaps. For instance, the partnership auction one club — one heart — one spade — three clubs was poorly defined. The range of three clubs was roughly 10-16 points and "mostly" forcing. Well, mostly forcing is like mostly pregnant; it is or it isn't.

Edgar sought systemic distinctions between the 10-12 point range, invitational, and 13-16, game-forcing. He conceded that the old-school approach got the message across without adding conventions. What could be clearer than a ringing three clubs in pear-shaped tones to force partner to bid, or a sulky, look-away three clubs that could be passed. (Bidding boxes had not yet been introduced.) Edgar hoped to embarrass the old school, but his main thrust was to convince experts and administrators that bridge would be a more satisfying and more challenging game if the Old Black Magic were replaced with intellectual, bridge-skilled solutions. Gradually, experts and administrators got on board with his plea.

One of the first was Roger Stern, Chairman of the Proprieties Committee in New York and one of the authors of the *Laws of Duplicate Bridge*. Roger was a crusader for improved ethics; one of his proposals was a mandatory ten-second pause by the third-hand defender before playing to trick one. The type of situation that he was trying to remedy was this: At notrump, West leads a fourth-highest spade deuce. Dummy follows with a low spade from queen-nine-three. East's spades are king-ten-eight; his correct play is the eight. This play stands to gain a trick if declarer holds ace-third or ace-jack-third, and it breaks even if declarer is dealt jack-third or three low.

A problem arises if East plays the eight after apparent thought—perhaps this is an unfamiliar suit combination. The pause implies that East had a choice, therefore holds a high honor, which he had considered playing. Imagine that West has led the deuce from jack-fourth and later gets the lead in some other suit. East's eight is consistent with ten-eight-low or eight-low-low, in which case declarer started with ace-king-low, and there is no future in returning a spade. However, if East's spades are king-ten-eight, a spade continuation will produce extra tricks for the defense. The tempo fluctuation at trick one creates unauthorized information (UI) that could assist West and damage North-South, innocent parties.

Roger's proposal would provide East with a 10-second grace period in which to plan the play without tipping his holding. Ideally, both automatic and problematic plays would appear in the same tempo. It was revolutionary for its day and still hasn't gained wide acceptance, although today's tournament directors and committees routinely attempt to prevent players from benefiting from UI.

Roger also instituted the Recorder process. In the early 1970's, I served as New York City's Chief Recorder. The idea was to create a vehicle where players could file complaints about conduct and ethics without confronting opponents. If an opponent bids or leads out of turn, call the Director to make a ruling. If an opponent gloats after a good result, or acts nasty after a bad one, call the Recorder. The Director is empowered to adjust scores by invoking the Laws. Bad behavior doesn't result in a score adjustment, but it needs to be addressed. The Recorder is sent a form, detailing the complaint, and he investigates the matter.

In most cases, education is what is needed; the Recorder, a tournament official, explains to the bad actor what standards are expected. This mechanism discourages players from accusing each other when there is unpleasantness at the table, and it improves the general level of behavior.

If your opponent displays dubious ethics, such as staring at his partner during play, fill out a Recorder complaint instead of accusing your opponent of cheating. Later in the session, the Recorder will take your opponent aside and explain why staring is considered improper—information is supposed to be transmitted by calls and plays, not the manner in which they are made.

In the rare case where opponents may be signaling illegally, the Recorder gathers evidence that can be used at a later hearing. If your opponent makes a wild bid or anti-percentage play that works like a charm, seek the Recorder. The Recorder will interview your opponents and form an educated opinion about whether they are poor players who happened to get lucky, or advanced players who may be using improper signals. If the players are unskilled but lucky, there's no foul, and the next several times they take outlandish actions, they rate to get bad results.

If the players are nefarious, the Recorder files will be useful if these opponents leave a trail of suspicious successes. The Recorder files were only to be opened at a hearing when the defendants had the opportunity to defend themselves—the idea was to avoid the appearance of a police state gathering incriminating data. The Recorder system in New York worked so well that the ACBL eventually adopted it both to instruct and to monitor.

The Bridge World did much to instruct directors and tournament committees in how to rule on cases involving UI, the most common type of complaint. The first step was for the Laws to explicitly state that capitalizing on UI is an infraction. UI results when the manner or speed of an action conveys information. A typical case: West opens one notrump and North has a problem that takes him a while to resolve. Eventually, his judgment tells him to pass. Has he done anything reprehensible?

Not at all; bridge is a difficult game that requires thought. However, North's pronounced hesitation before passing conveys that he holds a hand that is almost worth an action. On paper, a pass is a pass is a pass. When it is very slow or fast, it transmits extra information, but this additional information is classified as unauthorized, and its use by partner is not permitted.

It is unethical for South to take advantage of the UI. South is permitted to act when he has an obvious action, but he must pass, rather than bid or double, in a marginal case. The idea is to prevent players who huddle, inflect, or make faces to profit from their actions. Discrediting the Old Black Magic puts the emphasis on bridge skill. Once players are educated in what constitutes proper ethics, the great majority readily conform, and everyone finds it a better, more pleasant game, with fewer accusations of "sharp" practice.

Today, when you buy an entry to a national event, you sign a waiver, allowing the tournament organization to photograph you. Cameras are discreetly positioned around the rooms to film players at random. The idea is to produce visual evidence if anyone files an accusation of cheating. The cameras act as a deterrent, part of their purpose.

Tournament organizations have been forced to confront the proliferation of electronic devices. Cell phones in the wrong hands allow a cheat to send advance information about the deals to other players, presumably receiving the same in return. To ward off this modern threat, electronic devices were originally barred from the playing area. The revised ACBL policy is to allow the devices, but they must be turned off and out of sight; this restriction applies to any area connected to the playing space.

The threat of improper exchange of information is not new. When I started playing in knockout teams, if a player wished to visit the bathroom during play, it was not uncommon to be escorted by a tournament official or an opponent of the same gender. The chaperone's purpose was to prevent teammates from conferring behind stalls. Some people will try anything to win.

No question, tournament bridge has been scrubbed, sanitized, and bleached of almost every old blemish. Education is ongoing and thorough, bidding boxes are routine, and screens are seen in the late rounds of all major events. If a player produces a brilliancy, it is assumed that he managed it without illicit help. But it's a bit similar to the city fathers of New York allowing Disney to clean up Times Square, eradicating "The Bucket of Blood" in the process. Clearly, gentrification is seen as a benefit to the community and widely hailed as a boon to tourists, although some European cities have retained storied red light districts, precisely to attract tourism. In any event, local color has been sacrificed. Of the anecdotes of yesteryear that I'm about to relate, I wonder how many would take place in today's austere environment?

*   *   *

A high-school kid sits down against John Crawford and Tobi-as Stone, master intimidators whom you've already met in this book. The kid opens three clubs. Stone turns to him, "Are you old enough to preempt? Do you have any idea how many mas-terpoints there are at this table?"

After the kid goes down a few in his three-club contract, he turns to Stoney. "If you knew how few masterpoints I have, one of you geniuses would have doubled."

*   *   *

Andy Gabrilovitch and Jan Stone strike up a successful part-nership. Husband Tobias Stone is bridling with jealousy. "You two have an unconscionable edge. Neither of you would know a problem if you saw one."

*   *   *

In the days when an annual tournament was held at Asbury Park, NJ, it was common for North-South to be supplied with rattan rocking chairs. When a take-no-prisoners expert sat North, he bought two bottles of Coca-Cola, standing one near each edge of the table. When confronted with a tough guess, he would get his rocker going and knock off a coke bottle at his left or right, depending on which opponent's hand he needed to clip.

*   *   *

Andy Gabrilovitch is declarer in six clubs. His partner, Jim Linhart, the dummy, is close to seven-feet tall and lanky. Hold-ing a trump suit of ace-jack-ten-fourth facing dummy's king-nine-fourth, Andy leads the club jack, fishing for the queen. The Little Old Lady in second seat ducks promptly. Andy stews, then asks dummy to use his judgment. Nothing happens. The L.O.L. says to dummy, "Didn't you hear him say to use your judgment?"

Linhart, utilizing his height and long neck, duly picks off the queen, making the slam.

The L.O.L.'s partner turns on her. "Why did you ask the dummy to use his judgment?"

"I knew Mr. Gabrilovitch was an expert, but I didn't know about the dummy."

*   *   *

Al Roth, a savagely ethical expert, and his amateur partner are defending a slam. Declarer leads the jack of trumps from jack-ten-nine-fifth towards dummy's ace-king-fourth. In second seat, the amateur gives a convincing imitation of a player with a problem before playing low from two low. Declarer, taken in by the charade, ducks in dummy, and Roth ducks with queen-doubleton!

At the end of the deal, the mystified amateur asks Roth why he didn't take his trump queen and set the slam.

"You took so long to duck, I thought *you* had it."

*   *   *

A frustrated expert and his girlfriend are playing East-West in the Mixed Pairs with decidedly mixed results. In the middle of the session, a board is passed to the next table, and the West slot is crammed with ripped shards of cards, stuffed inside, with some tumbling out. The players who have to play this board are at a loss and call the Director who ambles over to where our hero, West, is sitting, still fuming.

"How did your cards get like this?"

"I dropped them and they broke."

*   *   *

Bobby Jordan finds himself playing against an old man with palsy. The man's hand shakes so badly that, despite Jordan's best efforts, he can't help seeing the old man's cards. Jordan needs to guess the queen of trumps, and he has seen that the man's hand is queenless. Confidently, he leads low from dummy and finesses his jack. The old man, still with shaking hand, reaches into his breast pocket and pulls out the trump queen. With the palsy magically gone, he takes the trick and gives Jordan a big wink.

*   *   *

Ivan Erdos and Jan Stone are playing together, and Jan is declarer at five clubs. To make it, she needs to lead dummy's singleton diamond towards her king-doubleton, hoping that the ace is onside to generate a useful discard in a side suit. This is not a difficult maneuver, especially for a player of her caliber, but, uncharacteristically, she fails to find the play and eventually goes down one.

"Don't worry," she says to mollify a steaming Ivan. "We'll get a good score because they're cold for four spades."

Ivan gathers himself. "Jan, I'll make a deal with you. Don't talk to me about bridge, and I won't try to explain childbirth."

CHAPTER 8

THE BRIDGE WORLD AND MONEY BRIDGE

If one publication has consistently represented the pinnacle of bridge, it is *The Bridge World*. Founded in 1929 by Ely Culbertson, the foremost authority of his day, it has provided a springboard for some of the game's most influential writers. A high proportion of the game's significant advances first saw light in this magazine. It covers the most prestigious tournaments in depth, analyzing the actions of the world's best players. It is the kind of publication that no aspiring expert can afford to be without.

I've been privileged to be a staff writer for over a decade under Editor Jeff Rubens. Jeff is a writer's dream. There are no real deadlines or restrictions on subject matter. His feedback invariably results in a much-improved article. I virtually never present him with a first draft, because I respect his exalted standards. Even after I have labored industriously, he finds significant ways to improve the piece, and other writers enjoy similar experiences. It's impossible not to improve your writing and clarify your thinking by working with Jeff.

Alphonse (Sonny) Moyse was the Editor from 1955–1966. Anyone who values superb writing and wit should read back issues from that era. Moyse and Albert Morehead, who succeeded Culbertson as Editor and doubled as bridge columnist for *The New York Times*, set a literary standard that has hardly been eclipsed. The magazine represented the cutting edge of advancements in the game, even though Moyse and Morehead's views were decidedly traditionalist.

Sonny, in particular, was an ardent fan of the four-three trump fit, a holdover from the four-card major days. He never tired of lambasting the Young Turks for their insistence on the sanctity of five-card majors and eight-card fits, and their swoon over scientific bidding. There are numerous deals where a four-three fit is the best contract, even at the game-level, occasionally for slam. Sometimes, declarer needs to understand how to manage four-three fits, either to maintain trump control or to scramble tricks, but here's a simple illustration that almost plays itself. The bidding is the key.

NORTH
♠ Q J 2
♡ 9 8
♦ A 9 3
♣ A Q 6 5 2

SOUTH
♠ A K 7 4
♡ 10 5
♦ 10 4 2
♣ K J 9 3

North deals and opens one club, South responds one spade. North's best rebid is two spades, not two clubs or one notrump. Average players love to rebid five-card minors; experts rarely do. North's raise with three-card support is the expert's choice, holding a ruffing value (short hearts) and quality in the raised major. South tries for game with three clubs, North bids three diamonds to show a stopper for notrump and suggest that he lacks a fourth spade. At this point, South knows to avoid three notrump. If North couldn't bid notrump on the previous round, neither player owns a heart stopper.

The remaining issues are to decide between a spade or club contract, partscore or game. Awareness of the power of strong four-three fits now comes into play. If South insists on clubs, the partnership had better stop at the four-level because five clubs can't be made. The game with excellent chances is four spades. If a player has learned to embrace the four-three Moysian fit, he can visualize the play and jump to spades.

The defense may cash two hearts and shift to a diamond, but declarer simply draws trumps. As long as spades divide no worse than four-two, a spade contract yields the same 10 tricks as clubs, with five club winners, four spades, and one diamond.

*   *   *

Near the end of Moyse's editorship, the magazine sponsored a historic match between the Scientists and the Traditionalists. Three top-flight pairs from each camp were chosen to play a lengthy team match. The Scientists could play any conventions they chose, but the Traditionalists were restricted to a small handful of conventions, Stayman, Blackwood, and little else. The idea was to test the effectiveness of modern (1960's) bidding. Moyse was clearly a Traditionalist rooter.

The Traditionalists jumped off to a very big lead, and old-timers were preparing their "I told you so" speeches. However, the Scientists rallied, not only wiping out the large deficit but winning by a convincing margin. Evaluating the results, Moyse took the position that poor judgment cost the Traditionalists the match, not lack of system. Edgar Kaplan, the next Editor of the magazine and a Scientist, made his case that "poor judgment" was a byproduct of poor system. If lack of conventions leaves a player guessing, even the best players will often guess wrong.

The players on the losing team admitted to being in bad form during the second half. The winning players thought that the team with the better methods won, as they had predicted. Not too many minds were changed, but the spectacle was highly entertaining.

In two subsequent Scientist-Traditionalist matches, in later years with different players, the Scientists also emerged the winners. Somehow, it's not surprising—good methods trump poor methods.

Moyse was no fan of the many conventions (e.g., negative doubles) that were infiltrating the game and the go-slow approach of a modern, forcing style. He always championed his causes with vigor and charm, but he knew he couldn't and shouldn't block progress.

Through my father, I was invited to Sonny's weekly home rubber-bridge game in the early 1970's. Sonny had suffered a slight stroke and was no longer active with the magazine, but his mind and wit were as sharp as ever. His hands were impaired, so the game was five-handed. The player who sat out held Sonny's cards, and Sonny, sitting over his shoulder, announced his bids and plays. The game was usually all-expert for stakes that kept those involved on their toes.

Situations arise in rubber bridge that seem foreign to duplicate. Partscores carry over from one deal to the next, altering bidding strategy. If your opponents are carrying a 60-point partial, one notrump on the next deal will give them game; consequently, you may be inclined to compete aggressively at the two-level. This policy is often carried too far. The best time to sacrifice is before they score a partial, which means duplicate strategy is applicable. Balance at low levels when they have shown a fit and limited their hands. If you are West and the opponents have 60 on score and bid:

SOUTH	WEST	NORTH	EAST
1 ♡	Pass	2 ♡	Pass
Pass	?		

balancing is very dangerous. South may hold 20 points and pass two hearts, because it is enough for game.

The general lack of close partnerships in rubber games, plus the inherent variety that bridge can generate, suggest that improvisation is a valuable skill. This is true for all forms of scoring, as noted in excerpts from an article in *The Bridge World*, December 2006.

THINKING ON YOUR SEAT
BY AUGUST W. BOEHM

In the theater, when something goes wrong, actors are expected to react instantly and improvise. Suppose a performer misses an entrance, leaving the rest of the cast temporarily in limbo. Someone on stage is apt to repeat the cue line; if that fails to produce an entrance, the onstage players must make up some dialogue or stage business until the tardy actor (or the stage manager) comes to their rescue.

On the concert stage, if a memory lapse occurs, the performer may begin to repeat passages, hoping for a light bulb to go on. One famous anecdote involves a piano-violin recital featuring Fritz Kreisler and Sergei Rachmaninoff. Kreisler lost his place in the Beethoven sonata they were performing and edged over to the piano, asking in a stage whisper, "Where are we?" Ever helpful, Rachmaninoff grumbled, "In Carnegie Hall."

How does this connect to bridge? Sooner or later, each of us will encounter an unexpected situation—indeed, in bridge one expects the unexpected. No amount of preparation can ready a partnership for every eventuality, so it is useful to cultivate the ability to think on your feet, or, if you are a bridge player, on your seat. To demonstrate different types of new experiences, I've collected a few oddball situations from actual play and offer them first in quiz form:

(A) Imps (with a regular partner); both sides vulnerable. Holding:

♠ K 8 2 ♡ 8 3 ◇ A K 7 3 ♣ K Q 5 4

you open one notrump; partner's four-heart response is a Texas transfer to spades; RHO doubles. Do you have anything to think about?

(B) Matchpoints; your side vulnerable. You hold:

♠ J 10 5 4 ♡ K J 9 7 2 ◇ A 10 9 2 ♣ —

Partner opens one club; RHO injects three notrump, which, judging from your hand, is presumably based on solid-looking clubs and some outside values. You double (or do you?); after two passes, RHO removes to four clubs. What now?

(C) Matchpoints; the opponents are vulnerable. You hold:

♠ Q J 3 ♡ J 7 2 ◇ A J 3 ♣ 9 8 7 5

LHO opens one notrump (15-17); partner intervenes with two clubs, showing an unspecified one-suiter; RHO tries three notrump. Any ideas?

On (A), after a four-level (so-called Texas) transfer, there is little utility in differentiating two-card support from greater length (as there would be facing a two-level Jacoby transfer, where both the degree of fit and the security level are uncertain).

What might well matter is the opening lead. If you routinely complete the transfer, LHO will lead a heart, and if partner has a heart holding such as ace-queen or king-low, your side will then be at a potential disadvantage. Why not pass the double, inviting partner to grab the four-spade contract if he has a heart holding that needs protection? If he has nothing in hearts, he can redouble as a retransfer (commanding you to bid four spades). This particular maneuver seems safe from disaster. Partner may not maximize his opportunities, but the final contract won't be four hearts doubled.

On (B), where RHO created a nuisance with his three-no-trump preempt over partner's one-club opening and his subsequent four-club runout, a pass is clearly forcing, given your penalty double. What about that penalty double of three notrump? It would have been more effective to have had available a "Gambling Three Notrump defense," perhaps where both four clubs and four diamonds show the majors, with the lower bid being stronger, as it permits opener to reply four diamonds with slam interest. Absent any such agreement, though, bidding four of a minor is very dangerous. From partner's perspective, either of those bids could be natural, especially if both of his minors are jack-high, masking the location of the notrumper's long suit. With limited partnership agreements, double seems appropriate: it shows strength and can hardly be misunderstood.

Now that you've doubled three notrump, should you pass the next decision to partner? When faced with uncertainty, that is usually wise. However, can you reasonably expect partner to co-operate intelligently? Would he bid a moderate four-card spade suit, or show a three-card holding in hearts? If he doubles, will the penalty offer adequate compensation for your side's likely game (which may even be in notrump—picture partner with, say, jack-ten fourth of clubs)? Here, also, it would be nice if four of a minor would be interpreted as pick-a-major, but couldn't it easily be natural?

It is responder's onus to gamble with four hearts. The hand is more distributional than average, and opener's high cards presumably lie outside clubs, improving the chance of picking up a heart honor or two. In addition, the auction is apt to help declarer during the play. Whatever happens, the unusual preempt and lack of a prepared defense has left you awkwardly placed, scrambling as best you can. It won't be the last time.

In (C), where partner showed a one-suited overcall of a one-notrump opening and RHO jumped to three notrump, you held an unprepossessing, balanced hand with scattered values. A pass is easy and noncontroversial, but what inferences are available? The jump to three notrump is apt to be based on a long suit—you can account for at least 24 HCP between your hand and opener's; if RHO has a balanced 10-count, partner is left with at best a very scrawny overcall. Besides, with a strong, balanced hand, RHO might have chosen a wait-and-see strategy, reserving the possibilities of a penalty double or a lebensohl-type sequence to check for stoppers once intervenor announces his suit.

If these inferences are sound, dummy's long suit is a favorite to be clubs, because your diamonds are much stronger than your clubs; with an 8-9 HCP hand including long diamonds headed by (at most) the king-queen, responder would probably only invite game instead of bashing into it. A fairly complete picture of the deal is emerging: RHO has six or more clubs headed by at least the ace-king. That leaves partner very short in clubs; so, whatever his long suit, your hand represents offensive gold—a good fit with meshing honors—and the vulnerability is favorable. How will you fare on defense? Perhaps your side can run partner's suit, but even when that is possible, will partner always lead from his length? Especially at matchpoints, he may prefer a safer off-suit start rather than leading away from, say, king-queen sixth of diamonds.

If RHO is an uncomplicated soul who might hold a square hand, you should probably pass and hope for a plus. However, if you can rely on your reconstruction of what RHO is likely to hold, you should bid rather than pass. How can you elicit partner's suit? Normally, bidding notrump in competition asks intervenor to show his length (like in response to a Michaels cue-bid), but four notrump here would cost a level. The best shot seems to be four clubs, which you hope will be read as pass-or-correct. But even if partner doesn't get the message and passes, you should be well-placed. If the opponents double, you can redouble (S.O.S.), clearly for takeout. If RHO decides to defend against four clubs undoubled, the opponents can't collect enough to offset their vulnerable game (even down 10 costs only 500). The full deal:

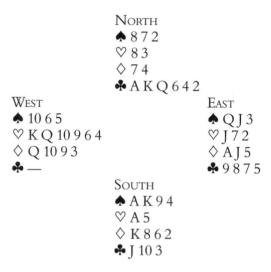

NORTH
♠ 8 7 2
♡ 8 3
◇ 7 4
♣ A K Q 6 4 2

WEST
♠ 10 6 5
♡ K Q 10 9 6 4
◇ Q 10 9 3
♣ —

EAST
♠ Q J 3
♡ J 7 2
◇ A J 5
♣ 9 8 7 5

SOUTH
♠ A K 9 4
♡ A 5
◇ K 8 6 2
♣ J 10 3

As it happens, three notrump is laydown, and four hearts produces at worst a down-two sacrifice (on a diamond lead from North), maybe even a plus score if the opening side perseveres to four notrump or five clubs, down on the normal heart lead; normal, that is, after your enterprise.

How successful were you on this quiz? No matter what, you will have acquired some additional experience in dealing with the unexpected. In most such cases, your approach ought to vary considerably, depending on the expertise of the other players or the solidity of the partnerships. This demonstrates that flexibility and adaptation are critical components of thinking on your seat.

*　　*　　*

Rubber bridge has fallen by the wayside. Many of today's younger experts may never have played a single rubber. Their feeling is that luck of the deal plays too large a role, and without regular partnerships, good bidding is compromised. These reservations are accurate, but they overlook other ways that rubber bridge can make a good player better. Rubber bridge with rotating partners forces a player to be flexible. Not all good players think alike; read a bidding forum and see how the expert panel is often divided. It definitely helps to become adaptable. This is useful when shopping for new partners, and it helps when playing. An expert must think along with an opponent; at the rubber bridge table, one grows acquainted with a variety of expert and non-expert strategies.

Rubber bridge also taught me another good lesson. No matter how thoroughly a partnership has discussed system, situations inevitably arise that are new because bridge is so vast. In such a circumstance, it is losing strategy to try for perfection when there is danger of a misunderstanding. Not all experts think alike. You may construe a sequence one way, but partner could be on a legitimate, yet different, wavelength. It is better to be practical and make calls that partner comprehends than to try something esoteric that may lead to disaster.

Rubber bridge builds character, because money is involved. If you compete for masterpoints and commit errors, the errors don't have the same impact as when your mistakes cost you, and your partner, money. When the stakes put you under pressure, you learn to handle pressure, or you find another pastime. Bridge is a lark for many, but important tournaments are pressure cookers. Sustained concentration is required for prolonged periods, and there isn't any physical release. Furthermore, no one likes to look bad when the intellect is involved. In athletic sports, as a person ages, it is natural to resign oneself to a loss of speed or strength. If you lose a senior tennis match, the damage to your ego is apt to be less than suffering a mental trouncing in bridge, regardless of age.

Rubber bridge also teaches you how to handle weak partners, a necessary skill if you play professionally, as I do. The Regency Whist Club, currently the only private rubber-bridge club that I know of in the United States, was recruiting junior members in the 1970's. A friend heard that the Club was discounting its initiation fee to attract young members. At the time, the Regency was renowned in New York City for the quality of its food, served in a beautifully appointed dining room in its East 67th Street townhouse, complete with a bar decorated in Parisian murals. The roster of members included several world-famous experts, such as Sam Fry, Boris Koytchou, and Harold Ogust.

My application for membership was declined. In fact, it never reached the Admissions Committee. Sam Fry, the club president, decided that I was too strong a player. He treated the weak rubber games as his personal fiefdom, and Sam didn't want to divide the lucrative pie with a newcomer. Later, I discovered that Bill Root, who had every desirable credential, was turned down for the same reason.

In those days, the admissions process to the Regency Whist included a written test. After the usual screening that Admissions Committees conduct, the applicant was given a written test, including some bidding problems and a hand or two to play. The idea was to determine the applicant's level of skill and his speed. A slow player is anathema to a rubber bridge table, where many contracts are claimed and overtricks are relatively insignificant. The Regency discouraged poor players who would cost their partners money, and the combination of poor and slow play was deadly. Such individuals drove players away from the club.

I did become a member of the Regency Whist Club in the mid-1980's by marriage. The club has an interesting history. The current townhouse was built in 1904 as a private residence.

In 1936, it was sold to a group headed by Mrs. T. Charles Far-relly, formerly a hostess at London's exclusive Crockford Casino Club, and opened its doors as The Regency Club in October, 1936. In 1964, The Regency Club and The Whist Club merged into The Regency Whist Club.

Early members included bridge greats and greats from outside bridge. Howard Dietz was one of the latter, the Director of Publicity for Goldwyn Pictures and credited with conceiving "Ars Gratia Artis" (Art for Art's Sake) and the lion as part of Goldwyn's logo. He was the lyricist for the Broadway hit *The Band Wagon*, and he wrote the lyrics for *That's Entertainment*, earning him inclusion in the Songwriter's Hall of Fame.

According to legend, he was challenged by a member of the Regency to write an impromptu lyric rhyming "Cyd Charisse," the high-stepping, leggy dancer, to the tune of "Jealousy." Dietz sat down at the club bar and whipped off the following lyric:

Cyd Charisse,
Get off of the mantelpiece.
It's quite a shock there,
We need a clock there.

George S. Kaufman, Broadway writer and director, who earned two Pulitzers and a Tony, enjoyed bridge at the Regency, even though his partners often provoked him. When a man, whose bidding had confounded Kaufman all afternoon, asked to be excused to visit the bathroom, Kaufman quipped, "For the first time today, I know what's in his hand."

On another occasion, Kaufman's partner badly misplayed a contract, going set when it was virtually laydown. "How should I have played it, George?"

"Under an assumed name."

When I joined, the Regency was dedicated to rubber bridge at varying stakes, with two duplicates a week. There was a formal dress code, but not everyone's behavior would have suited the

Queen. Rubber-bridge players tend to be excitable. Partner's gaffes cost both of you money, and, in the average game, there are plenty of gaffes. The Regency's barmen saw heavy duty, and the alcoholic consumption ratcheted up the players' excitability.

The club had a house pro for decades named George Rowe. If three members arrived and wanted to play, George made the fourth. He rotated in and out of tables, as needed. George was one of the Regency's memorable characters. He played better bridge drunk than most do sober. How is that possible? If a player has enough experience and natural ability, he can function capably on automatic pilot. A couple of George Rowe stories:

George is playing in a duplicate that I'm directing. It is well along in the evening when I notice an empty seat; it belongs to George. I ask George's partner, Archie, where he is. "Bathroom." Time passes, still no George. I venture to the men's room and remind him there are still a few rounds to play. When we return, George, weaving and suspicious, eyes me and Archie.

"That's not my partner." George and Archie have played together for decades.

"It's okay, George," I soothe. "It's Archie."

"Well, if you say so, but I prefer my regular partner."

We got George seated, and he and Archie finished the evening. They won by a landslide.

On a different occasion, George had finished his afternoon duties and was headed down one flight of stairs to freshen his drink. He miscalculated and toppled over the banister, landing with a thud on the roof covering the front desk. There was general alarm, but George dusted himself off and entered the bar, "Carlos, that shook me up a bit. Better have another Dewar's."

Robert Brimberg was another Regency character. Nicknamed Scarsdale Fats, he ran a brokerage house based on a unique business model. He would stage elaborate lunches at top-tier restaurants, supply the finest wines, and invite experts from the financial sector to speak during lunch about their specialty. The other invitees benefited from the speakers' remarks, as did Brimberg, and all he asked in return was that the invited firms run their stock transactions through him. Bob loved bridge and music, and he became a friend. When invited to someone's home for dinner and bridge, he usually brought a wicker basket containing a few goodies like goose liver, caviar and a Haut-Brion from a good year. He was splendid company.

Tom Smith was not a Regency member, but he belongs in this section. For years, he was the house pro and, later, manager of New York's famed Cavendish Club, not as swell as the Regency, but the place to play if you wanted to meet the greatest concentration of experts. Tom was an expert who enjoyed his bourbon, and he and I played from time to time as partners and teammates. One year, we dominated the Player-of-the-Year titles in the New York unit; he was the overall winner, I was second, and in the Team-Player-of-the-Year, I was first, he was runner-up. We were partnered on a team for the New England Knockouts. We had earned a bye for Friday afternoon, the first round. Tom and I were sharing a room, and when I arrived there was a Jack Daniel's bottle on the dresser, half empty. Tom greeted me warmly.

We reviewed our system and headed for the playing area. In the crowded elevator, the bourbon fumes were overwhelming. When the door opened, one of the players let out her breath. "I pity the person who has to be his partner this evening." Not to worry; Tom played very well, and we won in a breeze.

A final bridge and booze story: when Rabbi Richard Margolis (Columbia, "The Bucket of Blood") led a congregation in New York City, we played quite a bit of bridge together. By then, masterpoints had long lost any allure, so we sought other venues. One of the duplicate clubs staged midnight Calcuttas. This Calcutta was a pairs event and was well-attended; bridge players tend to be night owls. The bettors, who might also be players, bought pairs at an auction preceding the game. Richard and I always invested in ourselves, and we made a nice profit over the year.

Our trademark was to bring a bottle of VSOP Cognac to the game, set the bottle on the table, and sip throughout the evening until the wee hours. In the early rounds, before the Cognac had a chance to take effect, our opponents trusted our bidding and sometimes took phantom saves when we bid game or slam. Later in the evening, the Cognac seemed to disarm our opponents who thought us tipsier than we were, and they unwisely tried to take advantage, making risky bids. Despite the Cognac, we still knew how to double and defend. I doubt we could manage this feat today, but, in our thirties, we had the stamina to pull it off.

I don't for a minute mean to imply that bridge and booze (or drugs) are a good mix. When I accepted invitations to play in Cavendish Calcuttas, the players were world-class, there were tens of thousands of dollars at stake, and the only drink on any table was water or coffee. Some very experienced experts can play well by rote, but they would play better sober and, eventually, age catches up.

The world of money bridge has produced a motley lot. Gamblers are colorful; masterpoints don't attract the same sort of people. Not all gamblers are roguish; the Regency Whist Club housed a private game for astronomical stakes that included an equal measure of business tycoons and top-level bridge experts. One renowned tycoon described a good year he experienced at the bridge table when I chatted with him around 1990. The following portion of the conversation is verbatim; it was that memorable.

"You can't imagine the fun I have in that game," he reported. "I pulled off a memorable squeeze against one famous pro, and I hoodwinked another with a timely falsecard that made the *Times* bridge column."

"Over the year, how much money did you win? I asked.

"Win? In that game, me, a businessman, against all those experts? I lost a quarter of a million dollars, but so what. I had the time of my life and I came in *under budget*."

*   *   *

Edgar Kaplan succeeded Moyse as Editor of *The Bridge World* and remained so until his death in 1997. Edgar was renowned in every area of bridge. He was an expert player, an administrator, a bidding theorist, a witty commentator, and an authority on the Laws. I got to know him personally, first through the connection with my father and through music. Edgar was a frequent visitor to the townhouse on West 94th Street where his partner and system co-inventor, Alfred Sheinwold, lived with his wife, Elizabeth (Betty). Betty was a teacher at a local music school; she and Alfie (a tenor) and Edgar shared a love for classical music. I had the opportunity to be piano accompanist to both Betty and Alfie, and sometimes Edgar joined our ensemble on the flute.

The Kaplan-Sheinwold partnership suffered a serious rift when Betty divorced Alfie to marry Edgar. A New York tabloid quipped that a "bridge ace had trumped his partner's queen." Eventually, the men resolved their differences, and Betty had the rare accomplishment of celebrating two twenty-five-year anniversaries.

For many years during the 1970's and 1980's, I was a frequent guest at the Kaplans' house for their Friday night imp game. Edgar and Betty hosted, joined by three other pairs. Each pair played one match teamed with every other pair. At first, my father was my partner; later, Mike Engel. The stakes were gentle but not insignificant, the competition was strong, the hospitality warm and gracious, and the highlight of the evening came at the end when we shared a post-mortem of the deals and listened to

Edgar's commentary, invariably wise and witty. An invitation to that game was prized, as you can imagine.

Around 1990, I got the notion to interview some of the legends whom I knew personally. I didn't imagine publishing the interviews; for one thing, I couldn't tell if the results would be worthwhile. It was for my own pleasure and to have a permanent record. Edgar was the first I approached. He didn't seem keen to submit to what might be a lengthy session; by then, he had been interviewed by everyone under the sun. I got an idea—Bob Brimberg had left behind a superlative Bordeaux for a special occasion, and I knew Edgar's taste for fine food and wine. I called him and suggested an evening interview, and I would bring a Chateau Lafite. There was a momentary pause, "Okay, I'll make the dinner."

At West 94th Street, we had a deeply-flavored, dark veal stew that Edgar had prepared, we decanted and sipped the Lafite, and I turned on the tape recorder I had brought. The excerpts that follow from *The Bridge World*, August 2006, provide a glimpse of an extraordinary man.

EDGAR KAPLAN
THE BRIDGE WORLD INTERVIEW

Edgar Kaplan, who was Editor and publisher of The Bridge World for over 30 years, was a standout in many areas of bridge: player, coach, captain, theorist, author, commentator, legislator, and administrator. This interview is constructed from conversations with Augie Boehm during the early 1990's.

A.B.: What got you interested in bridge originally?

E.K.: My parents played; I learned watching them. My first partner was my brother, who was two years older.

A.B.: When did you realize that you wanted to make bridge the central part of your life?

E.K.: After the Second World War, I was at school at Cornell, and I started doing well in tournaments in that area; but I never had the notion that I played well, because I was extremely conscious of my own errors, which was probably one of the reasons that I got better. I didn't develop an ego about my own game until I got back to New York and started playing at the Cavendish Club, against players whose names I had heard all my life, bridge luminaries. What I discovered was that they played as badly as I did.

A.B.: When did you decide to turn your ability into a livelihood?

E.K.: It was a combination of circumstances. I was in business with my father and playing a lot of bridge. Then I won the Vanderbilt Cup, which was a great thrill. I felt very calm and composed in the last quarter of the final match. One of our opponents was Helen Sobel, the arch-rival of my partner, Ruth Sherman. We compared scores with our teammates, and we won. I wanted to get up and kiss Ruth, and I found that I couldn't get out of my chair, physically incapable of rising. It turned out I had been under some pressure after all.

A.B.: What have been your biggest gratifications and regrets over a lifetime of bridge?

E.K.: Gratifications are winning and regrets are losing. The biggest gratification was winning when I entered with no expectation of winning, when we played with Ozzie (Jacoby) in the Reisinger when he was old and dying from cancer. He had been very good to me when he was a great man and I was a kid. I think God wanted us to win. He even arranged for Eddie Kantar to revoke (which has probably never happened otherwise) on the last board to enable us to win. It was a popular victory, but most popular with me.

A.B.: The world of bridge is populated by so many bright and highly individualistic people, society might wonder about the game's social utility. Do you have any regrets about things you might have done had you not been so involved with bridge?

E.K.: No, I'm sure that my decision to concentrate on bridge was right. To spend my life at what I enjoy doing and at what I do well, that had to be right, even if there were financial incentives the other way. Some people told me I should have been doing something more substantial, but that is nonsense. They had difficulty understanding my perspectives that they were simply playing a different game for different prizes, and that my field had greater social utility than theirs.

A.B.: Over the years, changes in equipment and physical training have increased performance in many sports. How does that apply to bridge?

E.K.: There are many more partnership understandings now than before, but I'm not sure that is a major factor. In fact, I'm not sure that the best players now are stronger than the best players of an earlier generation. The best partnerships today are more practiced, so they are more effective. In the early days, you weren't married to a partner; typically, if you were on a team you had two or three partnerships with teammates.

There has been a progression. When I started playing, the best players were from a group that had come from auction bridge. These people were marvelous card players—largely in self-defense, because they were such lousy bidders. In fact, they were mostly not that interested in bidding; their energies and skills went into card play.

Today's young players put their energies and skills into bidding; they are not that much interested in the kind of creative defense that was seen, say, 30 years ago. The highest level of defense is when a defender tries to create an illusion in declarer's mind. And the most difficult case of that is where both partners must behave exactly as they would if they held a different hand. That kind of thinking was fairly common in expert partnerships a long time ago, but not today. People's interests have shifted towards methods, signaling partner accurately.

Similarly, the supreme declarers of yesteryear created illusions to hoodwink defenders. That doesn't happen much today. Today's declarers are thinking more about their problems than their opponents' problems. Most of today's declarers are technically oriented but not all—Jeff Meckstroth has some of the quality I've been describing.

The really big difference in the game today is among the second and third tiers of experts. These are much closer to the top players, so close there is very little difference. In the old days, there were very few good teams. For a while, one of two teams won most of the major knockout championships. Now, there is very little difference between, say, the top 20 players and the next 80, and only moderate differences between those 100 and the next 400. In the old days, the corresponding 400 could hardly play at all.

A.B.: Which modern methods or practices, if any, have favorably influenced the game?

E.K.: I don't see much importance in the particular bidding methods one chooses. What is important is to talk things over with your partner. The chief merit of using an unusual system is that it will force you to have extensive partnership discussions. Norman (Kay) and I have been playing for 40 years. We haven't discussed everything, but we do know how each other's mind works, so we can handle some auctions we haven't discussed.

A.B.: What are the key issues facing bridge administrators?

E.K.: One question that keeps coming up is the regulation of conventions. We have allowed the game free development; we want that—it is part of the American creed. To what extent should we allow players to invent their own methods without regard to the comfort or pleasure of other players? What should be done about the advantage that new methods gain purely through their novelty? Liberty and fairness conflict. Starting restrictions now would in effect say that perfection has been reached, or what I do is good and what you do is bad or evil, all obviously nonsense.

A.B.: How would you advise a would-be champion today?

E.K.: I would tell young world-beaters to forget about the bidding and put creative energies into card play. That is what modern players miss out on by not coming to tournaments from rubber bridge. When your father (George) started, his training was rubber bridge and his cunning went into card play.

A.B.: How have preempts changed over the years?

E.K.: In my youth, I had the reputation of being a wild man because I would open a three-bid with seven to the queen-jack-ten when the prevailing standard was king-queen-jack-seventh and an outside ace. I am very stubborn, and today I open the same preempts I did as a youngster, but I am now viewed as a dinosaur, because I won't preempt on jack-sixth.

A.B.: Have you clocked the effectiveness of your preempts?

E.K.: I haven't kept statistics, but I do review my results at the end of every session, and I do it in detail when records are available—it's a terrible penance to go over the records when you have lost a late-round knockout match. Any series of bad results with a certain type of bid or strategy stood out.

A.B.: What changes have you made as a result?

E.K.: One thing I decided against was bidding on a weak, distributional hand if I couldn't bid very high. Say RHO opens one diamond, and you hold five spades king-ten, two low hearts, queen-and-one diamond, and ace-fourth of clubs. Almost all American experts would overcall one spade. I discovered that by doing this I would lose in various ways. Primarily, we wouldn't buy the contract, and the opponents would have information about my hand. Secondarily, I would lose when partner would take me seriously and get us overboard. Then, he would "learn his lesson" and fail to compete appropriately when I had a sound overcall. I decided it was better to pass than overcall.

Anyway, as a result of study, the direction my game has taken over the years is towards not acting rather than acting on weak hands. If I can preempt, I preempt.

A.B.: Certainly modern players preempt more than old-timers. Could this be because bidding methods have improved, so there is more to gain by disrupting the opponents' auctions?

E.K.: But the preempt can help as well as hinder. A typical result is that a preempt pushes the opponents into some silly contract that they would not have attempted otherwise, then lets them make it.

A.B.: When preempts were more reliable, the preemptor's partner was often the only one who knew who could make what.

E.K.: Yes. The notions of captaincy have disappeared in modern-day preempting. You don't know what your partner has.

A.B.: It seems paradoxical that in earlier times bridge was considered more of an individualistic effort, yet in today's partnership-oriented world captaincy has been downgraded.

E.K.: There are really three identifiable generations of bridge players. The earliest generation, through the 1930's and 1940's, wasn't involved in captaincy. To people like Mr. (B. Jay) Becker, there was no such thing. He reserved the right to decide what was the winning action. The attitude of mind was to do what is right. In the second generation, from the 1950's and 1960's, and even the early 1970's, the players coming up then, people like Larry Rosler and Roger Stern and Jeff Rubens, followed different kinds of theories; to them, captaincy was critical. To people of my generation, if you preempted, you did not bid again unless you were right; to them, if you preempted and bid again uninvited, you were a fool regardless. It's a different attitude of mind.

*   *   *

Jeff Rubens took the world of bridge by storm in his early twenties. He was one of the leading Young Turks in the 1960's who were revolutionizing bidding. Before he graduated from Cornell, *The Bridge World* started publishing his series of articles titled "Bridge in Wonderland," a heady blend of whimsy and Olympian-level deals. You can read more about him (and Kaplan and Moyse) in the Hall of Fame section of the current *Official Encyclopedia of Bridge*.

I first encountered Jeff when I was at Columbia and he was co-writing the "College Bridge" feature for the ACBL *Bridge Bulletin*. The "Golden Oldie" deal, mentioned earlier in this book, originally took place in my college years. When I phoned the cards and auction to Jeff, within five seconds he asked, "What made you decide to play for the transfer squeeze?" That set me back on my heels. We might be hot-shot collegiate players, but there were miles and miles to go before reaching that level of lightning, spot-on analysis (if ever).

Jeff and I share an interest in Broadway musicals, and when I was assembling new material for *Bridge to Broadway* (2004), I asked him to contribute a parody lyric. He whipped off two; one from *The Mikado*, a number called "A More Judicial Devil" using "A More Humane Mikado" to dispense hellish justice to flouters of rules and ethics, and a parody of "There is Nothing Like a Dame" from *South Pacific*. I used the latter at the top of the show, and it got the evening off to a sparkling start.

Chorus:

When we won the Open Pairs
We scored seventy percent,
And we pocketed the prize pool,
(No more trouble with the rent.)
We had throw-ins, an elopement,
And a trump coup was a breeze,
What did we miss?
There was no squeeze.

We preempted laydown slams,
We were doubled into game,
Locked declarer on the table
When he made a bogus claim.
We remembered all our methods
And we knew which kings were keys.
What didn't show?
We had no squeeze.

Solo:

It's no thrill to win a few finesses,
Anyone can make some lucky guesses.

Chorus:

There is nothing like a squeeze,
Nothing in this world
Brings opponents to their knees
With the majesty of a squeeze.

Though our names are on the cup
Still our work seems incomplete,
Being high up on the list is
Just one reason to compete,
It takes art as well as science
Our aesthetic sense to please,
We're ill at ease
When there's no squeeze.

Tenor Solo:

Many plays in bridge are beautiful, but somehow . . .
There is one particular form that is head and shoulders
above the rest
And always makes me want to say—"Wow!"

Chorus:

There is nothing like a squeeze;
Nothing in this world
Brings opponents to their knees
With the majesty of a squeeze.

Key change:

No one ever disagrees;
Nothing in the game
Brings you joy of the degrees
When you execute your first squeeze.

Bass Solo:

Absolutely nothing can give guarantees–
Like a squeeze.

Chorus:

So suppose the count is wrong,
Or the solid suit is blocked,
Or you're short a dummy-entry,
Or your partner bid half-cocked.
It's a waste of time to worry
Over ev'ry last detail:
Play for the squeeze
And you can't fail.

There are some books on the squeeze,
An expert looks for a squeeze,
So always hope for a squeeze,
Prepare to cope with a squeeze,
Nothing works like a squeeze,
Has the quirks of a squeeze.
There is no day so poor it can't be redeemed
By just one gem of which we've dreamed:
A pseudo, brilliant, rare or incredible squeeze.

Not only is the lyric an encapsulation of squeeze technique, it conforms exactly to the meter and accents of the music. It also mirrors the dramatic arc of the original song, and it's funny. Jeff said he wrote it in "one take." I believe him.

CHAPTER 9

PROFESSIONALISM: BIG-TIME BRIDGE

A bridge professional is one who earns income by playing, teaching, writing, or directing, and I've been repeatedly engaged in all those areas. The history of professionalism is intertwined with the development of organized bridge. To survey the field, I've reproduced highlights from my recent series from *The Bridge World*, July, August and September 2012.

PROFESSIONALISM—PART I
BY AUGUST W. BOEHM

Professionalism in bridge, earning part or all of one's living through the game, covers many activities, but in current usage it is chiefly associated with playing for pay in tournaments. At the elite level, it has produced a game-altering impact. In today's Spingold and Vanderbilt knockouts, almost all of the top teams 1-16 include a sponsor, and a great majority of teams include top experts from outside the U.S.A. This trend extends to teams in the next 17-32 bracket; no longer can a top squad expect to coast deep into the event. Most observers agree that the influx of international talent, hired by wealthy sponsors, makes winning a national knockout much more difficult than winning the United States Bridge Federation's Team Trial, which determines the U.S. Bermuda Bowl representatives and is limited to U.S. residents. Some believe that it is even more challenging to win the Spingold or Vanderbilt than the Bermuda Bowl.

In Europe, tournaments offer substantial cash prizes. Prestigious invitational events like the Sunday Times and the Cap Gemini tournaments pay the pros' expenses to attend, plus the chance to win significant prize money. However, play-for-pay is uncommon outside the U.S. Consequently, foreign pros are willing to accept smaller fees than their American counterparts, making them attractive buys for a sponsor. Most observers agree that the addition of foreign experts to American events has created a higher standard of play, compelling all experts to practice and to study to remain competitive. Naturally, pros welcome professionalism—an individual is gratified to be compensated for expertise. Brilliant people who might have followed another career have become bridge pros, advancing the quality of the game, at least at the highest level.

Some observers argue that the probable presence of a playing sponsor on a U.S. Bermuda Bowl team weakens America's chances of a gold medal; the theory is that teams outside the U.S. are less apt to include a weak link (the sponsor). While this may have been true many years ago, it can now be argued that sponsorship in the U.S. enables compatible teams of the best players to devote their career activities to bridge, which bodes well for U.S. prospects in international competition. Besides, there is a prevailing view that many current sponsors are much stronger players than the sponsors of earlier eras; nowadays, some are clearly experts. In U.S. competition, teams with expert sponsors have a big edge over teams with weaker sponsors. Over the course of 32 boards, half of the typical knockout match, the errors of the weaker sponsor often decide a close contest.

In 1968, Dallas financier Ira Corn, Jr., formed the Aces, a team with the lofty purpose of restoring the Bermuda Bowl to American shores after a long run by Italy's Blue Team. The Aces had a coach, a trainer, curfews, and many hours of weekly scheduled practice; they used a computer to generate hands and analyze results. The players were salaried and received expenses. At the beginning, Corn was a playing captain; when he shifted his role to non-playing captain, the team prospered. The Aces went on to win the Bermuda Bowl in 1970 and 1971, a daunting mission accomplished, though eased by the temporary retirement of the indomitable Italian Blue Team.

In the 1970's, with the growth of professionalism in tournaments, the ACBL thought it advisable to take a stand and to protect the game's traditional amateur standing. At the grass-roots level, professionals and the sponsors who hired them were often resented. Disgruntled players who didn't hire pros felt unfairly outgunned. They reasoned, "Why should someone be able to buy masterpoints, Life Master status, or prestigious titles? Earn your way to the top."

A couple of laws were specifically aimed at inhibiting pros. Requiring the same methods to be used by both partners outlawed techniques such as one-way transfers (client North's two-heart response to one notrump shows spades, but South's shows hearts). Changing seats during a session was prohibited. Some pros sat themselves to a wild bidder's left, well-placed for a penalty double. Another strategy was to sit the pro, who would preempt if possible, to a timid opponent's right. Still other pros—and some expert non-pros—adjusted table positions, depending on who was the dealer, to enable the stronger partner to act first for his side in the bidding, slightly increasing that player's chance of becoming declarer. The average player's discomfort with these sharp practices, the fear that money corrupts ethics, and general resentment that pros were preventing average players from accumulating masterpoints, prompted the ACBL to take action.

In 1975, the ACBL established regulations for so-called Registered Players. According to the 2011 *Official Encyclopedia of Bridge*, "Any player who accepted money or other remuneration, directly or indirectly, in excess of actual expenses, as consideration for playing in an ACBL-sanctioned event, had to become a Registered Player." The thought was to identify the pros and to hold them to the highest ethical standards. A good many pros declined to register—no doubt income was going unreported, and it was considered unwise to create adverse vulnerability. Some observers asked why other ACBL members were not held to the same highest ethical standards. In due course, the regulation was repealed, perhaps because enforcement proved impossible.

*   *   *

PROFESSIONALISM—PART II
BY AUGUST W. BOEHM

By the 1980's, the ACBL was adapting to the expansion of professionalism. There was no longer any attempt to police activity at the club level, where many players seek to improve their games, and more-experienced mentors, often Flight-B players, offer to help for little or no compensation. Mentoring is clearly in the best interests of bridge and its organizations; instructing and encouraging new players in the clubs readies them for tournament competition. However, widespread professionalism at the club level, common nowadays and quite different from mentoring, can add a controversial component, especially if the client is a weak player and the pro's only objective is to score well.

In such circumstances, if the client's opening one-notrump range is 15-17 with classic shape, the pro's widens to 14-18 with a wide variety of shapes. Using Texas transfers, a pair is apt to leave a four-spade response to one notrump undefined—such a pair rarely introduces complexity to cover an infrequent hand-type. Accordingly, the pro may bid four spades to play rather than transfer with four hearts. In fact, a pair can decide to use Jacoby transfers but not Texas. When the client holds a six-card major and game-going values, he can transfer at the two-level and raise the pro to game. When the pro holds the same responding hand, he bids four of a major to play. This type of pro is trying to take the client out of the game, since it is in the client's best interests for the pro to declare. The goal is to simplify the auction and grab three notrump as often as possible, whether or not actions taken bear any relation to normally-correct bidding. The client learns little, but presumably that is the client's express wish—put my name in lights, win me some masterpoints.

If the client is primarily interested in learning the game, figuring that victories will follow, this objective must be made clear to the pro. This is the type of client I enjoy. The pro is willing to make client-level-appropriate bids and plays that shift the responsibility to partner; in effect, the pro tries to play real bridge.

For example, recently I held:

♠ — ♡ A 9 7 3 ♢ A K 9 6 2 ♣ A 10 9 3

Me	*Client*
1 ♢	1 ♠
2 ♣	2 ♢
2 ♡	2 NT
3 ♢	

Quite mystified—long auctions are generally difficult for inexperienced players—partner passed with:

♠ 8 6 5 3 2 ♡ K 5 ♢ J 10 3 ♣ K Q 4

so we missed a good five diamonds. Partner treated two hearts as a notrump probe, asking for a heart stopper, but when she confirmed a heart stopper and I retreated, she became confused and was unable to deduce my spade shortness and the power of her fit. (Her honor cards were all working, and she held no wasted strength opposite my shortness.)

A pro playing for score would probably bid two notrump over two diamonds, both to avoid subsequent difficulties and to become declarer at notrump. A pro playing to teach ought to pick two hearts; there may be a heart fit. This approach usually works poorly in the short run, but, in the long run, the client learns from mistakes, especially if learning is the client's stated purpose. Granted, some clients cannot learn. In that instance, the pro may as well play solo, but the habit of thinking solo can damage the pro's game when partnering a fellow expert.

In some clubs and sectionals, resentment, although abating, still lingers against professionalism and tends to be directed more against the sponsor than the pro, who is usually perceived as trying to eke out a living. Some players believe that a sponsor should be ineligible for masterpoints. I suspect that the structure of today's tournaments contributes to hard feelings. Players who began bridge in the era when most events had no masterpoint restrictions frequently encountered experts. It was an accepted fact of life, often welcomed. Today, tournament schedules condition average players to enter limited events without experts. When non-experts are forced to confront pros at the club level, where it isn't possible to segregate by ability, some feel victimized.

According to Michael Becker, a pioneer in the options-trading business who followed in the footsteps of progenitor Ron Rubin: "In 1977, Ronnie got into options trading, knew nothing, got tapped out, returned in 1978 with the proceeds of winning a backgammon tournament, took good advice from a backgammon-playing trader, learned to trade options based on their mathematical relationship to stocks, and became successful. In 1979, he trained and backed four bridge-playing friends (I was one), who were also successful—some of us sponsored and trained others. We were all in the right place at the right time."

Over the next decade, Becker trained, backed, or supervised about 100 traders, some 50 of whom played bridge—perhaps 15 were or became national champions. Other option traders with game-playing backgrounds included some top backgammon players, two top chess players, and a few blackjack card-counters. The bridge players made more money than the other games players. Becker notes that bridge and options trading require similar skills: coolness under fire; focus in the most-difficult circumstances; the ability to play well, whether ahead or behind, lucky or unlucky; the resilience to recover from mistakes; and gambling skills—never risk going out of business.

Ten years later, there were about 400 traders on the floor of the American Stock Exchange; about 125 were games players, and many bridge players did very well. The relevance of this success story to big-time bridge is that it spawned a generation of newly-wealthy bridge experts who began to sponsor teams in elite events.

Professionalism—Part III
by August W. Boehm

Play-for-pay applies to both sexes, although not equally. Below the top echelon, especially at the club level, there are as many women pros as men, if not more. At the highest level, men outnumber women, and there have been many more sponsors for the Open Teams than the Women's. Years ago, in the women's game there were one or two sponsors; now, there are several. In perilous economic times, the number of sponsors dwindles, and as the number of sponsors decreases, the pros' pay level is apt to go down. It's the fluctuating law of supply and demand.

Just as most businesses are reluctant to open their books to outsiders, some financial details of bridge professionalism are known only by the practitioners. As a rough guide, world-class pros receive $200-250 for a club game, although it depends somewhat on geography and the local cost-of-living. At a Regional, a top pro gets upward of $1,000 per day. At an ACBL national, the top pay is more than $25,000 for a ten-day tournament. What is general knowledge is that nowadays top-tier pros usually agree to contracts for cycles that encompass the three major ACBL team events and one Bermuda Bowl Trial. This was not always the case. In the mid-1970's, a sponsored team might be committed for only one or two major events. In the 1980's, it became common to sign teams for one-year cycles. Now, most sponsors of the top 16 teams make arrangements well over a year in advance, and many of these contracts are multi-year. Stability is encouraged. The pro receives a significant bonus for excellent performance. Sometimes, the bonus is stipulated in the contract; at other times, it is left to the discretion of the sponsor. The contracts may require regional dates, international tournaments, and Internet practice as part of a package.

As in the business world, personal relationships are meaningful, and there have been occasions where the sponsor has been more generous than the contract required. In contrast, some relationships go sour. There have been cases where the sponsor paid less than the agreed amount, paid late, or not at all.

The top female pros tend to earn less than their male counterparts. Their rates average perhaps two-thirds of what the men receive, in part because their team events attract a smaller entry. Fewer teams translate into fewer days, a shorter contract, and less money. However, it is also undeniable that the women's events are considered less prestigious than the open events, and this also accounts for the women's lower pay scale.

There are fewer professionals in the top-level of the women's game, making it more difficult for a female pro to find the right partner. If a pair is fired and not hired by a rival sponsor, whichever individual can land a job with another partner is apt to do so. Stability is rare; rosters tend to be in flux.

Only a very few top-tier teams of either sex have resisted professional attachments. Even when being paid is a minor consideration, being hired can be the only way to play on a team with other top pairs.

*

[*Author's note:* When I first started playing pro, it tried my patience, and I'm considered a patient man (some students say "saintly"). The way to keep my blood pressure under control was to revamp expectations. When I entered events with peers, I always thought I had a chance to win. Now, when I enter with some of my clients, expectations are dialed way down. I'm there to see that my partner has a good time and learns a little something. If we happen to score well, that's a bonus.]

*   *   *

From the client's perspective, Rabbi Leonard Helman wrote how professionalism enriched his bridge life. "Professionals elevate the standards of the game. They force amateurs to play at a higher level. My game improved when I started playing with pros. The fees are reasonable, not out of line with a high-quality evening of dinner and theater. The excitement of a high finish in a serious event could not possibly be available to someone such as myself without professional assistance."

Rabbi Helman offered a few pertinent pointers for the pros. "Encourage your clients. They want to learn but do not want their fragile egos crushed. Review all deals carefully. Praise whenever you can. Admit your mistakes. Pros who adjust to the occasion can be helpful at all levels of competition."

Amen.

CHAPTER 10

CLASS IS IN SESSION— THE LIGHTER SIDE

Of all the avenues open to a bridge pro—playing, teaching, writing, and directing—I've found teaching the most rewarding for both wallet and soul. The reasons are simple. The Card School and Bill Root business models, which are to develop and teach large classes, are more profitable than teaching an individual or a foursome in a living room. And since teaching is centered on helping people, with large classes you reach more people at one time. True, writing reaches an even larger audience, but the human response is nowhere near the same. You don't see, hear and feel people's joy when they grasp a concept, or make a difficult contract, or simply have a good time.

I've been able to carve out a self-employed life for four decades, and teaching bridge has been its backbone. My schedule is like an academic's; the peak periods are fall and spring. Winter, when many students travel south, reduces income but not work load, and summer is very low volume, which is when I do much of my writing and musical preparation. If there are some keys to being a good teacher, they involve being prepared, on time and presentable, a sense of humor, and a realistic idea of what can be accomplished. In this sense, teaching bridge is no different from teaching anything else.

I watched a few of the Card School professors teach, and I studied Bill Root when he was lecturing. Edgar was funny, urbane, and slipped some concepts into his intermediate lessons that even an expert could appreciate. Bill covered the waterfront;

167

he was as thorough as possible, all business, but with a genial air. I have tried to incorporate both approaches, adding my own style.

Teaching beginners is the hardest work I do. It's not easy to break every concept down into digestible bits. Even the language of bridge can be an obstacle. To some, "ducking" sounds like a play to be avoided—ducking responsibility is shameful. What about the gaffe of exposing your cards as the "dummy"? Wearing as it can be, teaching beginners is my way of returning something to the game. Once upon a time, we were all beginners.

When I teach most classes, I'm using only a fraction of my knowledge, but the challenge is to make a difficult subject accessible and enjoyable. When I'm able to meet that challenge, I leave class on a high note. Certain experiences are etched in my memory.

A number of years ago, a group of Japanese ladies, whose husbands were temporarily stationed in New York, engaged me for a series of lessons. The site was an apartment in Manhattan; I rang the bell and was admitted by a woman in a kimono and slippers. She gestured to me to remove my shoes before treading on the white wall-to-wall carpet.

Seated on the floor was a group of ladies whose chatter ceased the second I entered the apartment. The hostess bowed as she greeted me, leading us to the living room where the lesson was to take place. After a few moments, it was clear that either English or the bridge concepts were difficult for many of the ladies. The hostess would raise a hand to stop me, and the ladies spoke to each other in their native language. When the point I was making had been clarified, they motioned me to continue.

The entire lesson was stop-and-start, but it wasn't upsetting. On the contrary, I was getting a first-hand glimpse of how this group of Japanese ladies approached work. It was a group effort, the slowest learner was brought up to speed before she could become confused. In my Occidental classes, some students who understand the subject roll their eyes or flounce when another student asks what they deem a silly question. They hardly mind displaying their superiority, however unsubtle. In contrast, the Japanese always seemed to present a united front.

The lessons with Laurance S. Rockefeller and his wife, Mary, are another standout. I was recommended to them by a student and mutual friend, Peggy Nichols. I went to the Rockefeller penthouse apartment, was admitted by the butler, and we had our first of a series of lessons. The Rockefellers were strictly social players who thought they needed a brush-up. Both were down-to-earth people with a twinkle in their eyes, and we got along from the start. They had a keen appreciation of music, which helped. Eventually, I was invited to dinner and, later, asked to play cocktail piano at a party they threw. The piano was an old Baldwin grand in good condition with a specially de-signed Art Deco case. The party was nothing out of the ordinary, their regular caterer told me. The champagne that flowed freely was Cristal, and many of the guests were recognizable, house-hold names. The Rockefellers' private secretary had sent me a list of songs that were particular family favorites, so, of course, I played quite a few.

At one of my Carnegie-Weill recitals, I was programming Gershwin, and the Rockefellers took a whole row of tickets. As I was backstage, the Carnegie security man stopped by to visit. "There must be a VIP in your audience. Before the doors opened, I was asked to admit a private security agent to inspect the hall."

A bit later in life, another special class took place, although I didn't know it at the time. It was the first in a beginner series and a comely lady came up to me, introduced herself, and returned to her seat. Her name, Melissa Hubner. If teaching had brought no other benefits, this class would have made my career worthwhile. We were married, and the past two decades have been the happiest of my life.

*   *   *

When you teach a lot of students who never become good players, it is necessary to retain a sense of humor. It helps to remember that you are an entertainer, as well as a teacher. Here are some tales from my archives:

I usually follow the same format, a brief lecture on the day's theme, followed by at least four deals that I prepare. While the students play, I circulate, either to answer questions or just to get an idea of what's going on. Are my lessons sinking in?

One table was doing something odd that I didn't pick up, but it made my dizzy. Curious, I wandered over for the second deal. They were playing counter-clockwise, and they were in the third year of an intermediate class.

In some of the more socially-oriented classes, there is a fair amount of chatter from the students while they play. One afternoon, the silence was, in itself, unusual. I detected a faint snapping sound but it wasn't card-related. I couldn't identify the sound, but I figured out where it was coming from. At the end of class, I approached the table and raised an eyebrow. "Oh, that sound," replied one of the ladies. "It's me, snapping the waistband of my pantyhose. It throws the other players off."

At a supervised play session, declarer in three notrump correctly establishes a long suit in dummy. In dummy for the last time, instead of cashing the long-suit winners for nine tricks, she leads something else. It doesn't matter—the defenders contrive to let her make three notrump, then congratulate her on her success. She asks me if she did anything wrong. I show her how she isolated herself away from dummy's winners, converting a then-laydown contract into a struggle. She nods thoughtfully: "It all makes sense. When I was growing up in Greece after the war (WWII), we had no paved roads. I had to learn to get where I was going on gravel."

I am teaching Mrs. Cyrus Vance, wife of the former Secretary of Defense under President Carter, one-on-one at their apartment. I bring Mrs. Vance deals that she can declare. She always holds plenty of high-card points and enjoys herself. After several months, I broach the subject of playing against some live opposition. She agrees that it's a good idea and arranges for another couple to be present at a subsequent lesson.

In preparation, I suggest that we practice leads and signals because the opponents may play the hand. This possibility causes some consternation, but she composes herself and sighs. "I suppose you're right. My husband always preached the importance of defense."

During the play segment of a lesson, dealer opens the bidding one heart. Her LHO puts the nine of diamonds on the table. Responder continues the auction with three hearts. I am called to the table when fourth seat realizes that something isn't right. I take stock of the situation. "I hope you remembered to alert the nine of diamonds."

A couple gets into an argument after one of the deals. "Why didn't you return my diamond lead?" he demands.

Her retort, "I only had 3 high-card points."

A noted bridge teacher is enjoying a pastoral scene in the country. On a warm summer day, a mother duck is guiding her ducklings down the bank to frolic in the pond. The family seems ready to swim to the opposite bank when the mother grows alert and climbs back up the bank, craning her neck, this way and that, clucking with concern. Soon, her worry becomes evident—a duckling is missing. The straggler duckling emerges from the bushes and scurries over to Mom who hurriedly ushers her entire brood to safety.

The teacher reflects. Mother duck keeps better track of nine ducklings than many students do of five outstanding trumps.

After a duplicate, a pair ask me how they should have bid one of the deals. Their auction started:

$$\begin{array}{ll} 1\,\text{NT} & 2\,\clubsuit \\ 2\,\heartsuit & 2\,\spadesuit \\ 4\,\clubsuit & \end{array}$$

I ask opener about the four-club bid.

"It's Gerber."

"Why would a limited hand use Gerber, especially since partner denied game-going strength?"

"Because I had 21 high-card points and a singleton."

"Why did you open one notrump with 21 high-card points and a singleton?"

"I was afraid partner would pass if I didn't."

I'm not making this stuff up, and sometimes it gets to me. I return home one evening and Melissa asks me, "How was your day, dear?"

"I went to the dentist for a root canal and gave two lessons. The best part of the day was the root canal."

* * *

When I teach an advanced class or conduct a seminar, the level and pace is very different. The amount of time I spend on preparation is vastly different. Selecting interesting topics is crucial. Advanced players are enamored of conventions. Because they have learned to manage, if not master, the essentials, they feel ready for more. I'm ready to oblige, but I'm happiest when I can provide them with a more permanent tool—the ability to think logically. Except for concentration, logic is the most important attribute of a good player—"If this is true, then what must logically follow…?" Learning conventions is fine, using them well is even better, and improving card play technique to take your tricks is the most important because you use these skills every session, while a favorite convention may not occur during a month of frequent play.

The ability to approximate the thought process of an expert is invaluable to an aspiring student. To present an over-my-shoulder perspective is the point of the next article, excerpted from *The Bridge World*, May 2006.

ROTE VERSUS LOGIC
BY AUGUST W. BOEHM

Some students, perhaps a majority, learn best by emphasis on rote memorization, a recitation of rules; others find explanations of underlying and unifying principles more satisfying. Preferences seem to depend on educational background and even natural endowments. By the same tokens, some teachers are better equipped for one mode than the other. Making a value judgment, I find rote teaching to be of a lower order. How much skill is involved in teaching youngsters the alphabet? (Patience is a separate matter.) Find a catchy song, or a rhyme scheme, or some associative pictures, and both student and teacher are on the road to success.

Learning bridge, some students are taught to memorize a set of guidelines, perhaps aided by flash cards or catchy phrases (second hand low, third hand high, eight ever, nine never, etc.). With a certain amount of repetition and patience, many basic building blocks can be installed. And, soon, the beginning student will be up and playing, a worthwhile goal.

In contrast, explaining why these principles are generally effective and examining notable exceptions make greater demands of both teacher and student. If the student's ambitions are only moderate, then the shortcut rote procedure may be preferred, especially if the student is inclined to save headache, heartache, time and money.

Ultimately, though, the rote approach is severely constrained for developing real bridge talent. If ever a game were based on logic, that game is bridge, and pedagogies that eliminate or sidetrack the application of logic necessarily leave the student handicapped for later advancement.

A major culprit is blind reliance on point-count, and the use of rote memorization to promote point-count enslavement is particularly crippling. One of my pet peeves is to hear players who should know better describe a hand as "a 7-count." For one thing, the common hand-evaluation methods that produce "7 points" are egregiously oversimplified and distorted. For another, the implication that all hands that count the same must be worth the same is ludicrous, deadly to a serious player. The classification itself is gratuitous and prejudicial—7 points sounds weak. To be sure, books and teachers charged with instructing the experienced player know to shade and refine terms, but can a student raised on rote memorization be expected to profit from subtle modifications? Early impressions and habits are difficult to overcome.

Another serious shortcoming of the rote approach is that the student is impeded when applying knowledge in a foreign context. Consider a common convention, splinters. It is simple enough to teach the basics: an unnecessary jump is a splinter, typically describing a four-card raise of partner's last-bid suit, showing a singleton or void in the named suit, plus (usually) game-forcing values.

To derive benefit from this very useful device, one must understand how to react to partner's splinter. A hand with secondary honors (king, king-queen, king-jack, queen, queen-jack, jack) opposite partner's shortness contains wasted values; it is worth less than its point-count. A hand with purity in the short suit, just the ace or no honors, is more valuable than its surface count.

With just that much discussion, a student is sensitized to a hand's fluctuating value. If an instructor were to define comprehensively which jumps are splinters and to present plenty of examples, all would be ready for the launching pad, right? Well, not exactly.

One of my regular students picked up this collection:

♠ A J 9 6 4 3 ♡ A 9 6 2 ◇ 8 ♣ 7 3

Sitting opposite, I opened one club; the next player intervened with one heart; my student bid one spade; advancer raised to two hearts. I doubled, showing three-card spade support. We employ this technique, even when partner has guaranteed a five-card suit, to provide trump definition; doubling for penalty in front of the opponent's trump length at low levels has little utility. Intervenor passed, leaving my student in the driver's seat. Alas, a calculation of only 9 points facing what might be a minimum opener led to a two-spade rebid.

Many of my student's peers would likely have made the same call for the same reason. They play with their own professionals, and one teacher's approach, or misquotation, invariably leaches down to other teachers' students.

"9 points" is language I avoid, but still my students fall under its spell. 9 points? This hand bears as much resemblance to an ordinary nine-point hand as the Grand Canyon does to a drainage ditch. Two defensive tricks, exciting six-four distribution with the boss suit, the possibilities of lead-direction and preemption, and an easy rebid add up to make this a mandatory opening bid in my book, and I don't consider myself a light opener.

As the auction actually developed, this nine-pointer became a colossus. With the opponents' overcall and raise, partner is likely to be very short in hearts. In effect, responder has encountered a splinter situation (albeit facing only three-card trump support). Applying hand-evaluation principles, we see that all the high-card values are working and even the minor suits are aligned well—with the singleton diamond in the unbid suit, the doubleton club is more likely to find its losers covered because of partner's opening one-club bid.

Write down a high-card minimum that partner might hold, including heart shortness, say:

$$\spadesuit \text{ Q 10 x} \quad \heartsuit \text{ x} \quad \diamondsuit \text{ A J x x} \quad \clubsuit \text{ A J x x x}$$

Even with the wasted minor-suit jacks, 10 tricks are easily in range by ruffing hearts before drawing trumps. Does this make four spades the correct call? No, because it is an underbid. Partner might hold:

$$\spadesuit \text{ K Q x} \quad \heartsuit \text{ x} \quad \diamondsuit \text{ x x x} \quad \clubsuit \text{ A K J x x x}$$

which furnishes a decent play for six spades. With slam potential opposite a modicum of extra strength, three hearts seems best. Perhaps it won't get the partnership to every good slam, but four spades will reach none of them. On deals such as this, a student whose early training stressed counting points starts several strides behind one who was encouraged when possible to visualize the play, or some aspects of it, during the bidding.

And this underscores the basic need to teach play before bidding, or, at the very least, alongside it. How can students be expected to understand what a hand is worth if they don't know how tricks are won?

Next, here's a problem-type where rule-bound students may fail even when they get the right answer! As South, you hold:

♠ J 10 6 2 ♡ K Q 7 6 2 ◇ A 9 ♣ Q 3

At matchpoints, with neither side vulnerable, East opens two spades. Do you take positive action? The hand strength and suit quality are sub-minimum for three hearts, and the spade length is a warning sign. Unless you find at least a four-card heart fit, you rate to be saddled with slow spade losers. A pass is in order, and only an in-tempo pass will preserve partner's options.

A player trained to think about the critical requirements for an intervention at a higher level will see immediately that this hand is not worth one; passing in appropriate tempo should not be a problem. A student at first distracted by the relatively high point-count, or opening-bid strength, may be able to reach the correct conclusion but faces the additional worry of tipping partner that there was something to think about.

In practice, the average player who faced this problem passed after considerable and obvious deliberation. The auction continued with West's bumping to three spades and partner's sailing in with four hearts. What would you do now?

That four-heart bid encompasses a very wide range, anything from a minimum opener with a long heart suit and a spade void to one of a number of powerhouse holdings. Regardless, your hand must be a great deal better than partner hoped to buy, loaded not only in trumps but also in the minors; partner rates to be short in spades.

I would vote for five hearts, ignoring the question of how partner would or should interpret a bid of five diamonds; when disastrous ambiguity is possible, it is best to find the answer to such a question only through later discussion. If partner has a spade void and grand-slam ambitions, he can continue with five spades—after that, a six-diamond bid will be unambiguous.

Unfortunately, the previous tempo disruption taints the auction. Having broadcast that he has some values, advancer may be able to infer that intervenor's four-heart bid is solid, because with a marginal hand the four-heart bidder would have passed to avoid taking advantage of the unauthorized information from the slow pass. Clearly, a player should not be entitled to profit from being the transmitter of unauthorized information. The situation is messy. It may seem unfair to blame such awkwardness on rote learning, but it is a fact that inferior education affects the game negatively in several ways.

Because I believe that rote instruction is the far inferior route to building good bridge players, I reject it, not only from personal preference but also because the logic-driven approach attracts the kind of student with whom I enjoy interacting. However, there is the business issue. One of the best-selling instructional devices ever developed was a laminated, two-sided card; it claimed to summarize all that anyone needed to know about bridge. It succeeded in an era when bridge possessed the potential for mass marketing—nearly every American enthusiast (and much of the general public) was familiar with bridge and played approximately the same game.

Nowadays, the "product" (bridge) is diffused. There is social bridge, online bridge, club bridge, tournament bridge, and strictly expert bridge. No longer does one size come anywhere near fitting all, and different approaches can be valid when they attempt to cater to greatly varying student needs. Thus, picking an approach to learning bridge is not so much a question of which route is superior as it is a matter of teacher and student together finding an appropriate vehicle.

CHAPTER 11

THAT'S ENTERTAINMENT

By now, you probably realize that bridge can be deadly serious and also lots of fun. Combining bridge and music is one of the best parts of my career. Over the past decade, I've been lucky to lead bridge seminars at private resorts in the Caribbean during the winter, and in Venice at the famed Hotel Cipriani during the fall. At the Hotel Cipriani, I play with James Sherwood who revived the moribund Orient-Express train in the late 1970's and purchased the Hotel Cipriani around the same time. The two investments coordinated beautifully. The train, fully restored by the early 1980's, ran from Paris to Venice. When passengers at the Venice terminus needed a hotel, before or after the trip, the luxurious Hotel Cipriani was at hand. This cross-pollination provided a springboard for the burgeoning Orient-Express hotel empire.

When Jim attends our bridge week, as is usually the case, he and I play as partners in the duplicates. He is great company, both at the table and away from it. On the final evening of a recent bridge week, he and his wife Shirley offered their private launch to take our bridge group to their favorite fish restaurant on the outskirts of the lagoon. Our party occupied the whole restaurant; the owner plied us with local wines and endless platters of seafood caught that morning, plus a decadent dessert called Sgroppino, an amalgam of lemon ice cream, Prosecco, and icy vodka, whipped to a froth in a blender and served in chilled glasses. I'm not sure that many of us recall the boat ride back to the hotel.

Jim is an interesting man. Kentucky-born, Yale-educated, he became an eminently successful businessman, making his first fortune from container shipping. In his autobiography, *Orient-Express—A Personal Journey*, he describes how bridge played a pivotal role in his life. He writes, "I played a lot of bridge at Yale, often well into the night, and usually for money, and my fortunes prospered." After Yale, he entered the navy and met a base commander who examined his Yale record and found that Jim was "an accomplished bridge player." The commander was looking for a fourth, Jim completed the officers' game, and after Jim left the navy, the commander helped Jim get started in the container-shipping business.

Jim concludes, "Without being considered a reasonable hand at bridge, I could never have bought the Orient-Express. So, in a way, it all began that evening at the bridge table." The legendary train continues to prosper, and the Orient-Express hotel chain is respected worldwide. If your travels take you to one of these delightful properties, offer a little prayer of thanks to the wonderful world of bridge.

At each seminar, I volunteer to perform a cabaret, singing and accompanying myself in traditional Porter and Gershwin songs, along with bridge parodies, many of them culled from *Bridge to Broadway*. Here are two parodies from the 2004 revival that audiences seem to appreciate the most. The first, "Oh, What a Beautiful Contract," is by Richard Margolis to the tune of "Oh, What a Beautiful Morning" from *Oklahoma*. The second, "Overbidder," is by Don Simmons, based on "Old Man River" from *Showboat*.

Oh, what a beautiful contract,
Our bidding was eager and strong.
I have a wonderful feeling
Nothing could ever go wrong.

There are five trumps between the defenders;
I'll extract them and make them surrender.
I lay down my ace with a smile on my face,
But a five-oh division now slows down my pace.

It's still a beautiful contract,
Nearly secure as before.
One little setback won't hurt me;
Surely I'll suffer no more.

There's a side suit to care for my loser,
But a ruff-in said, "That you won't do, sir."
I only had one but the defender had none,
And suddenly this contract's a little less fun.

I'm in a hopeful contract;
Still several things could go right.
I'll get proceedings back on track
Giving it one mighty fight.

There's a two-way finesse for a queen;
When I find her I'll feel really keen.
The count says go left and my play is quite deft,
But the queen's on my right and it leaves me bereft.

Oh, what a miserable contract.
How did we get up so high?
I can't escape the feeling
I'm just an unlucky guy.

*

Overbidder, that overbidder,
When he shows somethin',
It don't mean nothin'.
He just keeps biddin';
He keeps on biddin' along.

He don't pass signoffs;
He don't pass invites,
And with them that pass 'em
There's often been fights,
'Cause Overbidder
He keeps on biddin' along.

You and me bid down the middle,
Brain cells achin' 'til we find a bid that will
Gauge the risks, weigh the scales,
But deal him some junk
And he's off the rails.

I get weary, the strain's amazin';
I'm tired of passin'
And feared of raisin',
But Overbidder
He just keeps biddin' along.

*   *   *

The 2004 show also featured author Alan Truscott, *The New York Times* bridge columnist. Alan held that post for close to four decades, maintaining a consistently high quality of journalism. Born in England, a man of immense accomplishments, he was a British internationalist before emigrating to the United States. From my earlier chapter on cheating scandals, you may remember that Alan was highly instrumental in producing evidence against fellow Brits, Terence Reese and Boris Shapiro. Alan wrote a lyric for the show based on a Gilbert & Sullivan song. Best of all, he agreed to perform it. On cue, he strolled onstage in a tweed jacket with a copy of *The Times* under his arm, looking every bit the transplanted Englishman. We made a live recording of the event, unfortunately of rather poor fidelity, but I sent Alan a copy. He wrote back, "You get the highest credit for your key role as producer, director, pianist and singer, and "Overbidder" is my favorite. I confess I liked listening to myself and discovering that I was not as bad as I feared."

At our rehearsals, he shared an idea he had been contemplating. It was known that Stephen Sondheim of Broadway musical theater fame was a keen bridge fan, and an avid games player and puzzle creator. Alan thought to interest Sondheim in playing an informal match that would make good copy for his *Times* column. He asked me if I would be interested in such a project.

Would I be interested? "How soon?"

I was one of the many theatergoers who admired, or, in my case, revered Sondheim's work for the musical stage, both from the audience's perspective and from performing his songs in cabaret, as well as musically directing Sondheim shows in summer stock. Alan wrote Steve a letter proposing the project.

Sondheim demurred, saying that although he read *The Times* bridge column religiously, he was rusty, the other players would be too good for him, etc. Alan was not easily dissuaded. Gathering courage, he mentioned that New York was presenting a musical revue before a national audience of bridge players and he, Alan, had written a lyric, and the director of the show (me) was a bridge-expert-musician. Going to the brink, Alan wondered if he might show Sondheim his G & S parody for comments.

This did the trick. Sondheim replied, "If you have the temerity to send me your lyrics, I can summon the nerve to play bridge with you." Alan recruited a friend, Andy Arkin, who was an old friend of my father's and the high school bridge partner of Edgar Kaplan.

Alan partnered Steve, and I played with Andy. It developed that Sondheim, after some initial nervousness, was quite equal to the challenge, as you will see.

Alan had asked some cohorts to prepare interesting deals from a previous international match. The idea was that each of

our pairs would compare results against the internationalists, to
gauge whether we matched their par, or perhaps achieved a sen-
sational birdie, or regrettably dunked our bridge ball in the water
hazard. After the match, Alan scored the results and typed this
deal into his column that appeared on January 22, 2004.

West dealer
Neither side vulnerable

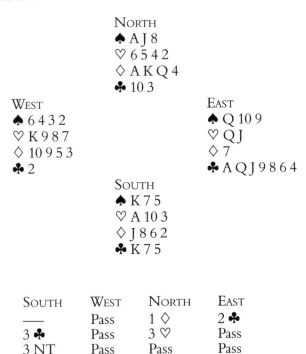

NORTH
♠ A J 8
♡ 6 5 4 2
♢ A K Q 4
♣ 10 3

WEST
♠ 6 4 3 2
♡ K 9 8 7
♢ 10 9 5 3
♣ 2

EAST
♠ Q 10 9
♡ Q J
♢ 7
♣ A Q J 9 8 6 4

SOUTH
♠ K 7 5
♡ A 10 3
♢ J 8 6 2
♣ K 7 5

SOUTH	WEST	NORTH	EAST
—	Pass	1 ♢	2 ♣
3 ♣	Pass	3 ♡	Pass
3 NT	Pass	Pass	Pass

North was Andy Arkin; I was South. My club cue-bid suggested an invitational raise in diamonds, and we maneuvered
into three notrump. Alan led a club, Steve won with his ace and
continued with the club queen. I won with the king, rather than
hold up, saving my remaining club to throw East on lead for an
endplay. If East had defended in routine fashion, the endplay

would have succeeded. When I run my diamond winners, East is pressured into finding three discards.

If East discards two clubs and one heart, South cashes the heart to remove East's last heart and exits with his carefully preserved low club. East can take three club winners but must lead a spade into dummy's ace-jack combination at the finish. If East decides to discard three clubs, the seven-card ending would be:

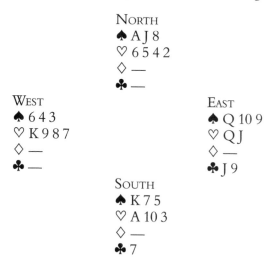

NORTH
♠ A J 8
♡ 6 5 4 2
♢ —
♣ —

WEST
♠ 6 4 3
♡ K 9 8 7
♢ —
♣ —

EAST
♠ Q 10 9
♡ Q J
♢ —
♣ J 9

SOUTH
♠ K 7 5
♡ A 10 3
♢ —
♣ 7

South can play the ace and a low heart, achieving a rare position known as a winkle. If West rises with his king, South's ten becomes a winner, and if West plays low, East is endplayed, forced to lead a spade after cashing his clubs. Declarer scores four diamonds, three spades, one heart, and one club.

This neat ending was never reached because, on the run of the diamonds, Sondheim threw a club, a spade, and another club. His effortless discards left declarer with a problem. As the cards lay, I could have played spades from the top, dropping the now-doubleton queen. Instead, convinced that the spade queen was on my left, I cashed the king and finessed the jack: down one. Well done, Steve.

After the match, we adjourned to Andy's club for drinks and dinner. Getting to meet Sondheim in person that evening led to other highlights. I had been mulling a Sondheim fantasia, a collection of his significant works arranged for solo piano to use in one of my recitals. Steve approved the idea, and the piece was programmed in concert and recorded live. When I corresponded with him, busy as he is, being in worldwide demand, to every letter I sent I received a reply within a couple of days. I once asked him if he was the best bridge player in the Broadway community. Modestly, he said that honor belonged to Arthur Laurents, the playwright and his collaborator on *West Side Story* and *Gypsy*.

*   *   *

Alan and Dorothy Truscott were frequent guests at the Kaplans' home imp game, and we met many times in tournaments, both as opponents and teammates. I feel I owe Alan a great deal, because he chronicled so many of my exploits at the card table, as well as introducing me to Leonard Pennario and Stephen Sondheim. There are other ways to get your name in lights, but a *New York Times* mention does the trick, and it helped promote my career. The Truscotts were a natural choice when I decided to conduct interviews of bridge celebrities for posterity. Alan died in September 2005, just before this interview (excerpted here) was published in *The Bridge World*, October and November, 2005.

DOROTHY AND ALAN TRUSCOTT
THE BRIDGE WORLD INTERVIEW

This is the first of a series of interviews with leading personalities that will appear in this magazine. Some date from 10-15 years ago, others from the present day. Augie Boehm couldn't resist a "two-fer," simultaneously interviewing Dorothy and Alan Truscott, two of the world's leading bridge personalities. Both excelled as players, writers, theorists, publicists, and good-will ambassadors for more than 40 years. These discussions, from which these excerpts are taken, date from the mid-1990's.

A.B.: What are the most significant differences between bridge as we approach the turn of the new century and the old days?

D.T.: Earlier, there was more joking. Players were less formal. Today, things like the Alert procedure have people worried to death that they may be doing the wrong thing, and they hardly ever open their mouths to say good evening.

A.T.: Certainly, in some ways behavior has improved. We no longer see the temperament and bad manners that affected some of the well-known East Coast players. Some of the most forceful personalities and unpleasant opponents are gone.

D.T.: If you had dropped out of bridge and tried to come back nowadays, it would be hard. There have been so many changes in methods over the years. Another very big difference is that now, to be effective, you are almost committed to work with one partner.

A.T.: Yes. The great teams of yesteryear used to switch around.

D.T.: That's why the Betty Kaplan Teams (an annual New York event, named for Edgar's wife, in which every player must partner each teammate for the same number of boards) is such a good idea.

A.B.: What about the quality of play now compared with back whenever?

D.T.: Bidding is much more scientific.

A.T.: Even in the 1930's, the top players played their cards very well. But their bidding was rudimentary. For example, Culbertson never opened one notrump, because he had not come up with a method of responding to it effectively.

A.B.: How do the top women play today compared with earlier decades?

D.T.: Better, and they are continuing to get better still.

A.T.: There is greater depth in the women's game today. Earlier, there were only two or three women's teams that had a chance to win a national women's team event; now there are many more.

A.B.: To what do you attribute this?

D.T.: It used to be that 90 percent of women players tried to look pretty, to be pleasant, and to attract some nice man; to say the least, they were not dressing to play bridge. Now, a lot more really think about serious bridge.

A.T.: And many more are willing to work on a partnership.

A.B.: Do women experts tend to be feminists?

D.T.: Few care much about it.

A.B.: Women have a choice between open and women's events. Is that good for developing strong women players?

D.T.: I think not. In the early days, I played in almost no women's events. Then, rules came in that for international women's team qualification you had to play on an all-female team and participate in women's events. That seems foolish, but perhaps it was better than the even-more-stupid rules that came earlier.

In 1960, there was a Women's Team Olympiad for the first time. The ACBL Board of Directors created selection rules in which any player who had done well in any national event in 1959 would be "considered." The Board then made its choices. I played mostly rubber bridge, but that year I had done very well in the Nationals, winning with Betty Adler and with Johnny

Crawford. So I was selected, even though I had never played a board with anyone else on the team.

Three of the selectees were relatively weak. The captain simply rotated everyone, which was foolish, because we had three strong players: Agnes Gordon, Helen Portugal, and myself. We could have won the event if given a chance. Helen Sobel was still active at that time, but she was playing in the Open. Unfortunately, Margaret Wagar had had a bad cycle in the 1959 Nationals.

In any case, it was bad for women's bridge when the ACBL made rules that women could get trial-qualifying points only if partnering another woman.

A.T.: In contrast, for a while there was a good rule that an all-women's team could get women's qualifying points for each match won in the Vanderbilt or Spingold, which both encouraged women to form partnerships and to play in those events—good experience and practice. Unfortunately, the League then scheduled women's events in parallel with the open events.

D.T.: Women should be encouraged to play in open events, not only in parallel women's events.

A.B.: How did you get started in bridge?

A.T.: In 1940–41, London was bombed regularly, and at school we were sent to air-raid shelters where we spent a lot of time playing chess and bridge. At the time, chess was my main game, bridge was my second game. I never dreamed that I would later give up chess, but two games plus job plus family was too much. Chess is an antisocial game; a teenager may be introverted and antisocial, thus more attracted to chess, but gradually becomes more social.

A.B.: Some chess masters have tried to take up bridge. Why have so few "gotten" bridge?

A.T.: There is a tendency to make too many decisions, something you get used to in chess, but bridge involves a partner.

D.T.: In my family, there was always a bridge game going on. From when I was seven, I was sometimes allowed to kibitz instead of being required to go to bed. At first, I pretended to be interested, just to get to stay up late, but then I sort of did get interested. One time, a guest was an hour late, and I was allowed to fill in. After that, I was hooked.

A.B.: You have each invented conventions that are now standard practice.

A.T.: I invented one of a suit—double—two notrump as a constructive raise. Tommy Sanders thought it was a great idea and mistakenly gave Bobby Jordan credit for it.

D.T.: I invented splinters [around the same time as the publication of the same idea by Dave Cliff—*A.B.*]. Alan told me about the English practice of using an unusual jump to show a void. I first suggested to B. Jay Becker, my partner at that time, that we use this void-showing device. He thought it wasn't worth the trouble. By way of argument, I said we could use it about seven times as often if it could also show a singleton. He dragged a leg for a while, but eventually we adopted it.

In the 1960's, conventions like that were considered major revolutions, and there was an esoteric approval process. Before we used splinters, Becker and I played in a trial announcing only Blackwood and Colorful Cue-Bids (one spade — two spades intervention shows red suits, etc.) on our convention card. Mr. Becker never liked the Stayman convention, though he did adopt it in later years. In this trial, Sam Stayman complained that we had not had Colorful Cue-Bids approved; he had the director bar it.

A.B.: He canceled half your system.

D.T.: Some restrictions were outrageous. Once Crawford opened a devastating 4-point weak-two bid against a member of the ACBL's Board of Directors, which led to the infamous 6-12 HCP rule (weak-twos had to fall within that range). I once held:

♠ K Q J x x x ♡ Q J ◇ Q J ♣ J x x

It didn't even occur to me to count points with a hand like that, but I had 13 HCP. I opened two spades in fourth seat, as did many others. At one table, someone called the director when the opener's hand was revealed, and the directors went around the room penalizing everyone who had opened two spades. After that, I guess the ACBL realized how stupid it looked, so the rule was finally changed.

A.T.: Inventiveness can be important outside bidding and play. To prevent pairs in a team match from sitting in the wrong direction, thus canceling all the results, place a slip in the first board of each set, giving the names and positions of each player. This is the Truscott card.

A.B.: Both of you have strong family connections. How do you account for the statistic that so many of the top bridge experts are not family-oriented?

D.T.: We are one of the few husband-wife pairs that can get along at the table; most don't even try.

A.T.: We had an established bridge partnership before we were married, which helped. I have formed the impression that no one will ever become very good at bridge unless he or she has submerged himself in the game at some point. When I was at Oxford, I absorbed everything I could—books, magazines, discussions. Once having experienced such a stage, one can play well without keeping up such an intense level of involvement.

A.B.: How much of your early training was in rubber bridge?

A.T.: Not so much of mine. For a few years I played some, but the majority of my sessions were always in tournaments.

D.T.: I played rubber bridge a lot. Mr. Becker played a lot of rubber bridge. We were horrified that his sons, Steve and Mike, never played rubber bridge. I wondered how they could ever get to be good without that experience, but they did.

A.B.: What do you think about screens and bidding boxes?

D.T.: They are marvelous.

A.T.: They dull the edge of people who would pick up little twitches from their partners. Aside from having a fairer game, it is much more relaxing to play behind a screen, because you don't have to worry about whether your demeanor will give information to your partner.

A.B.: What pithy advice would you give to a potential world-beater?

D.T.: Concentrate on getting the best out of your partners. I suggest being gentle.

A.T.: Find a partner of equal stature and work hard on agreements.

A.B.: Does that imply regular practice?

A.T.: Yes. Partners married to each other at least have that advantage.

A.B.: You two have won several national titles after switching to relay-based methods. Do you attribute this to system, luck, or increased practice regardless of method?

D.T.: Well, being lucky is important. People often self-destruct, typically with the last bid of an auction, giving away the luck they have been dealt. There is also the matter of overcoming one's deficiencies. For example, too often I try to sneak something through rather than pursue the technically best action. I always go for the swindle, both in bidding and play. That's bad.

A.T.: Be careful on the first and last boards of a session, where a very high percentage of serious mistakes are made. On the first board, you haven't settled down, and on the last board you are anxious to compare results.

D.T.: Be willing to accept advice. I remember reading an ancient Goren book that Blackwood is a device for keeping out of slams, not for reaching them. Gradually, I realized how insightful that remark was. No one ever believes this advice when I offer it.

A.T.: To be as effective as possible, you must train yourself to shut out everything else that is happening—noise, kibitzers, rulings at the next table, wondering what is happening at your teammates' table.

A.B.: But as a journalist, don't you need to be alert to all sorts of subsidiary matters?

A.T.: Yes, but the element of time pressure has receded; I can gather and use material much more flexibly. Nowadays, it is so much easier to file stories, which can be done electronically, that I have much less worry about timing and meeting deadlines. Computers have been an enormous advantage to me. I can write from home instead of always going to the office.

A.B.: Bridge has so many colorful stories, apparently because experts are brainy and eccentric.

D.T.: Once in a cut-around imp team game, my teammates were Sonny Moyse, Ira Rubin, and Tobias Stone. We had to decide our lineup. Sonny and I clung to each other, but Ira and Stoney said they would line up any way we wanted as long as they did not have to play with each other. After much haggling, I wound up playing seven boards with Stoney. I tried to "do nothing" and nothing happened. Unfortunately, I kept cutting him, and we wound up playing together again and again. I knew something big would happen, and finally it did.

He opened one spade, and I had a monster. I jumped to three clubs, forgetting that in Roth-Stone that was a weak jump-shift. He had such a big hand that even though he took three clubs as weak he bid three notrump. I assumed he realized that I had forgotten. Total disaster ensued, and, even though that cost a lot of money, I was kind of relieved when he swore he would never play with me again.

A.B.: What unusual coups do you find memorable?

D.T.: I opened six hearts twice in one day. Both should have worked right, but on one Howard Schenken ruined things by bidding seven, with two aces, opposite my voids of course.

A.B.: Do you have any special perspective of bridge?

D.T.: Bridge is a marvelous game and has been wonderful to us. We try to give back through pro bono promotions and talks.

A.T.: Some years ago, we tried to help the Russians organize bridge in their country. We raised money for them to travel across the United States to the Nationals at Seattle. It turned out that one of their main needs was for directing instructions. I managed to get Alex Groner's *Duplicate Direction* translated into Russian, and it was printed and distributed. We still have quite a few copies under our bed. Want one?

*

[*Author's note:* Alan and Dorothy collaborated on *The New York Times Bridge Book*, a survey of the game's history and some of its leading personalities.]

*   *   *

I'm coming toward the end of my story. To be sure, there were other personal adventures with connections to bridge history. I twice played in duplicates sponsored by the American Bridge Association (ABA), founded in 1932 to promote the interests of African-American bridge players. Blacks were not welcome in the ACBL until the early 1950's, and even after segregation bans were lifted, the ABA continued to grow, establishing a master-point system and conducting national championships, as well as local events. The ABA created its Hall of Fame in 2000, and their charity program offers scholarships and donations to causes like the Sickle Cell Foundation. Since the 1990's, the ABA and the

ACBL have acted to promote relations between the two organizations. I've played in ABA events in New York and on Martha's Vineyard, and I have found the ABA players unfailingly polite, well dressed, and informed about bridge. Nor was I the only Caucasian attending.

Writers who follow the bridge scene sometimes have particular interests. One, Nikos Sarantakos, keeps track of deals that set records. In his book with David Bird, *Famous Bridge Records*, Nikos claims that Richard Margolis and I tied a record in high-level competition for bidding and making a small slam on a combined total of only 12 HCP. I don't know what it proves, except that distribution can trump high cards, but it did take place against world-class opponents in the final round of the tournament calendar's toughest event, the Reisinger board-a-match teams.

The *Daily Bulletin* at the Boston NABC in 1999 ran this account:

THE WILDEST HAND

One of the most interesting hands to be seen on Vugraph was Board 23 from the evening session of the Reisinger board-a-match teams.

South dealer
Both sides vulnerable

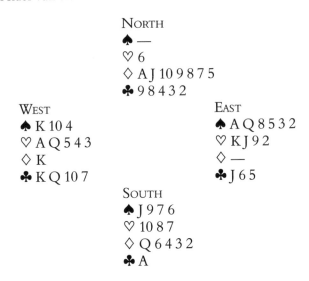

NORTH
♠ —
♡ 6
◇ A J 10 9 8 7 5
♣ 9 8 4 3 2

WEST
♠ K 10 4
♡ A Q 5 4 3
◇ K
♣ K Q 10 7

EAST
♠ A Q 8 5 3 2
♡ K J 9 2
◇ —
♣ J 6 5

SOUTH
♠ J 9 7 6
♡ 10 8 7
◇ Q 6 4 3 2
♣ A

The Vugraph commentators were having a ball with this one. It appears that East-West can make a small slam in either major. But what about North-South? Where are the losers if North-South play in diamonds? The only loser is a heart—six diamonds is cold. This is what happened when Augie Boehm and Richard Margolis held the North-South cards.

SOUTH	WEST	NORTH	EAST
Margolis	*Levin*	*Boehm*	*Weinstein*
Pass	1 ♡	4 ◇	5 ◇
6 ♣	Double	Pass	Pass
6 ◇	Pass	Pass	Double
Pass	Pass	Pass	

Making of course!

*

196

[*Author's note:* The six-club bid not only prepared the way for a successful defense, it altered the North-South captaincy situation. Our partnership followed traditional theory, where the preemptor's partner becomes captain, being well-informed to make all further bidding decisions for the partnership. Six clubs allowed the captain to offer a decision to the preemptor; if the opponents had continued to six hearts, I would have doubled to prevent partner from sacrificing. Then, I could have jump-started our defense with a suit-preference lead of the club nine.

A clinic in a single deal, and bridge at the top.

The Sarantakos-Bird book reprints this six-diamond deal with the headline: "Fewest points for a successful small slam," and adds a bit of commentary: "Look at that great lead-directing six clubs by Richard Margolis. It paved the way for a successful defense, should East-West advance to a small slam in hearts."]

*   *   *

Bridge historians are well acquainted with the Culbertson-Lenz match. In December 1931–January 1932, a challenge match was waged between Ely and Josephine Culbertson versus Sidney Lenz and his associates. Culbertson was the dominant force in bridge when the game was at the height of its popularity. Lenz headed a group of experts who were jealous of Culbertson's impact. Lenz & Co. felt they had the better system and the better players, and a grudge match was arranged.

It received phenomenal press coverage, in part because Culbertson and Lenz were striking personalities. When the long match was concluded, the Culbertsons had won by a decisive margin, and bridge was the beneficiary.

In 2002, Alan Truscott organized an event to commemorate this "Match of the Century." We played deals from the famous match, and the event was broadcast, not over the radio as in

1931, but over the Internet, thus around the world. Talk about having kibitzers! It was staged at the Waldorf-Astoria, which had hosted the second half of the original match. I referenced the match in an excerpt from *The Bridge World,* November 2003.

TEACHER'S PETS
BY AUGUST W. BOEHM

In January, 2003, I took part in an exhibition in New York that recalled the Culbertson-Lenz match. I played the role of Sidney Lenz. My partner for most of the match was John Kranyak, portraying Oswald Jacoby; Bobby and Jill Levin were the Culbertsons. Kranyak and I had never met until game time. Accordingly, I proposed that we play essentially convention-free, both to avoid misunderstandings and to replicate bridge history, where Lenz was the conservative standard-bearer and the Culbertsons were the New Scientists.

During the 18-board segment, we didn't once suffer from lacking a convention. In fact, we reversed history and outscored our opponents, thanks to good luck and a few scoring quirks. Significantly, a couple of deals would have troubled modern players who had removed all the traditional clubs from their bag.

For instance, with the opponents vulnerable, I picked up:

♠ Q J 9 8 6 5 3 ♡ 9 7 4 ◇ 10 ♣ 7 6

With our opponents vulnerable, my partner opened one diamond, and RHO overcalled one heart. I was glad to have a three-spade preempt available—our agreement was that if a call could be natural, it was. No, I wasn't blind to the tripleton in intervenor's suit and the singleton in partner's, but the vulnerability was favorable, my suit had texture, and it was spades, the genie in the bottle in competitive auctions. (In another era,

Adam Meredith worked wonders with the spade suit against world-class players.)

In our encounter, my preempt caught this layout:

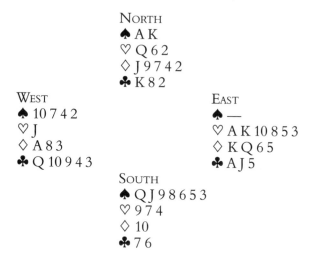

NORTH
♠ A K
♡ Q 6 2
◇ J 9 7 4 2
♣ K 8 2

WEST
♠ 10 7 4 2
♡ J
◇ A 8 3
♣ Q 10 9 4 3

EAST
♠ —
♡ A K 10 8 5 3
◇ K Q 6 5
♣ A J 5

SOUTH
♠ Q J 9 8 6 5 3
♡ 9 7 4
◇ 10
♣ 7 6

West, Jill Levin, passed; North passed; and East, Bobby Levin, reopened with a double, which West passed to net plus 300, a poor return. Yet, did anyone do anything strange? East's actions seems clear-cut, West's reasonable. The pressure of the spade suit worked its magic, controlling a level. Today's players use many competitive jumps as splinters, or as fit-showing. That works well on some deals, to be sure, but the inability to pre-empt in spades bears a hidden and high cost.

*

[*Author's note:* The scoring method was to compare our 2003 results with the original results, adding or subtracting points when the modern results were different. In most cases, it wasn't hard to equal or improve on the original. The Culbertsons and Lenz were among the strongest players of their era, but bridge has come a long, long way since 1931.]

*   *   *

I trust you've enjoyed meeting some interesting people in these pages, many of whom are ensconced in the ACBL Hall of Fame, and all of whom are indelibly imbedded in my memory. Memory is important to me, and I try to keep it well oiled with daily practice. Along the way, perhaps it has helped me to memorize hundreds of pages of music, or perhaps recalling bridge hands helps with musical memorization. My musical memory is the stronger, and it derives from many sources.

A few musicians are blessed with a photographic memory; they see the printed score in their mind's eye. Others learn by ear; their memory is grounded in the auditory sense. Still others have kinetic memories; like an athlete, muscle memory is the prevailing guide—the fingers just know where to go. For myself, I use a blend of all three, and I believe that is common. In any case, I don't remember bridge deals as well as I used to. Before there were computer-generated hand records, one was forced to rely on memory to engage in post-mortems after a session with partner and friends. Hand records are a great convenience, especially for writers, but they can make a bridge player's memory lazy.

If you're ever in Memphis or across the river in Horn Lake, Mississippi, drop into ACBL headquarters, visit the Hall of Fame museum, and learn more about the legends and history of this wonderful game. There is a lot more to bridge than shuffle and await the next deal. Knowing something about the history of the game and its leading lights heightens one's appreciation. It's no accident that bridge is the world's greatest card game, but it is facing a crisis if the ACBL is unable to recruit younger players.

Let me conclude with a couple of short, humorous pieces that combine my two loves, bridge and music, and, within the broad category of music, the poles of musical theater and opera.

When conceiving these articles, I think the idea is to start with a very good bridge deal or two, preferably with an unusual twist to complement the comedy in the text. Then, retain the storyline if one exists, remain true to the essential nature of the characters, and, when possible, try to incorporate the original tone, situations, and language. Let's start with *The Bridge World*, August 2012.

GUYS AND DOLLS
BY AUGUST W. BOEHM

Readers who want to keep apace with recent literary developments will be interested in the discovery of a hitherto-unpublished short story, attributed to one Ramon Bunion, similar to the stories that were the basis for the musical *Guys and Dolls*.

The action takes place when the New York police have confiscated all the dice in the city and established an embargo, leaving many Broadway gamblers at a loss, and none more so than Nathan Detroit, whose percentage from a roving crap game provided him a nice living. The Biltmore garage was available at a reduced price, so Nathan bought a suitcase of (unmarked) playing cards and circulated word that bridge had replaced craps. Nathan's game had a wrinkle: The stakes were affordable enough; the big money was in the side bets that players and kibitzers could place on the outcome of any contract, even during the play.

The news attracted the attention of the action-starved denizens of Broadway, especially Sky Masterson, who loved all betting propositions, the bigger the better (hence his nickname). He was falling in love with Sarah Brown of the Salvation Army Mission, but she wasn't returning his play. Meanwhile, Adelaide, Nathan's girlfriend, continued to lament her unmarried state.

And so it happened one Friday evening, in the Biltmore garage, Sky found himself partnered with Sarah Brown, hoping that his bridge acumen might break down her resistance. On his left was Big Jule (pronounced as Julie), a most unsavory character; on his right was Adelaide, playing under protest (Nathan had promised to play with her that night in the mixed pairs but pleaded business at the last minute): "Just make up a table and next week we'll head to Niagara Falls," he assured her. Skeptical but comforted by visions of mink, she acquiesced.

A syndicate was formed to back Adelaide, although this required Nathan to call in a lot of markers. Sarah presented a special problem: She hated gambling, so Sky spoke to Nathan beforehand. "My partner doesn't approve of betting, so could we arrange a code between you, me, and the others? If someone wants to bet, click a lighter once to bet a grand, twice for two grand, and so forth. I'll do the same if I'm taking the bet." Everyone beefed more than somewhat, maintaining that dolls and gambling are like Mindy's worst goulash, and, by the way, what was Adelaide doing here instead of singing at the Hot Box—but, eventually, out of regard for Sky, they agreed.

This was the fateful deal:

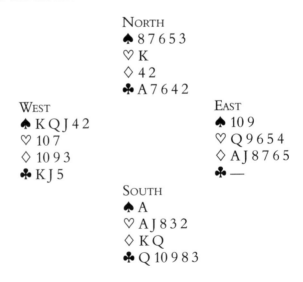

NORTH
♠ 8 7 6 5 3
♡ K
♦ 4 2
♣ A 7 6 4 2

WEST
♠ K Q J 4 2
♡ 10 7
♦ 10 9 3
♣ K J 5

EAST
♠ 10 9
♡ Q 9 6 5 4
♦ A J 8 7 6 5
♣ —

SOUTH
♠ A
♡ A J 8 3 2
♦ K Q
♣ Q 10 9 8 3

At the Biltmore, everyone was vulnerable at all times. Adelaide, East, the dealer, wanted to make a good impression on Nathan, so she started with a disciplined pass. Sky, South, opened one heart, and Big Jule, West, intervened with one spade; Sarah, North, passed, and Adelaide chirped two diamonds. Sky competed with three clubs, and Big Jule raised to three diamonds. Sarah, appreciating her distribution and two helpful honors, leaped to five clubs, passed around to Big Jule, who doubled—intimidation was his long suit. Now Sarah showed the stern stuff of which she was made: "Redouble," she said, and, looking directly at Sky, she added, "If you don't make this, forget about that trip to Havana you're planning and anything else."

Big Jule led the spade king. Sky won, unblocked dummy's heart king, and played a low club; his queen fetched the king, as Adelaide discarded an encouraging diamond. Big Jule won and switched to the ten of diamonds; Adelaide won and thought a bit before returning a spade—everyone knew that Big Jule was accustomed to living on his muscle; a little thing like a four-card suit overcall was of no consequence. Adelaide sighed when Sky ruffed with the nine. Declarer played the club ten, and Big Jule paused. His kibitzer and confederate, Brandy Bottle Bates, edged around the table to take a peek at Adelaide's cards; he could see that the hearts weren't breaking. With some quick finger motions, he sent both the duck signal and the bet signal to Big Jule. So informed, Big Jule sneered at Sky: "What do you think of your contract now?"

He clicked his Zippo once. (At this point, the reader might decide whether to defend or to declare.) Sky studied the proposition and clicked his lighter with a glance at Big Jule. The kibitzers crowded in closer. Brandy Bottle could see that Big Jule's jack of clubs would become the setting trick if Sky ruffed his three losing hearts. If declarer didn't pursue the crossruff, Adelaide's heart queen stood to become a winner. Lacking a lighter, Brandy struck a match. Sky nodded briefly in his direction and clicked once. Then, he cashed his heart and diamond winners and ruffed a heart, confirming the five-two split, while West discarded a spade. A spade ruff produced this ending, with South to lead:

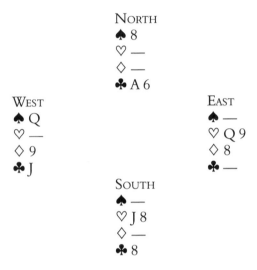

NORTH
♠ 8
♡ —
◊ —
♣ A 6

WEST
♠ Q
♡ —
◊ 9
♣ J

EAST
♠ —
♡ Q 9
◊ 8
♣ —

SOUTH
♠ —
♡ J 8
◊ —
♣ 8

Sky turned to his left-hand opponent. "I sympathize with your double, Big Jule, but unfortunately for you, I now have a sure thing." He led a heart.

West had no defense. A diamond discard or the jack of clubs would permit a crossruff, a spade would allow declarer to ruff low and to pull the last trump. Five clubs was made, doubled, redoubled, and re-redoubled.

Big Jule began to reach inside his coat for the old equalizer, but Brandy Bottle has halfway out the door; meanwhile, Adelaide was hoping that Big Jule wasn't about to criticize her defense.

Sarah was impressed by her partner's play, as well as his sportsmanship. "Well played," she murmured.

"And bravely bid," Sky returned, "You showed a lot of faith in me."

"What do you expect? I'm a Mission doll."

*   *   *

The last selection is from *The Bridge World*, January 2012.

GRAND OPERA
BY AUGUST W. BOEHM

It is not well known that fictional characters who die before the final curtain are consigned to the Void to await their next operatic production. And so Carmen, Salome, Scarpia and Tosca found themselves with time on their hands, playing bridge. Even the Void has structure; Carmen and Tosca were partnered against Salome and Scarpia, the pure versus the base. It was a one-table game with no comparisons and no stakes, so virtue or evil had to be its own reward.

NORTH
♠ Q 7 2
♡ 3
♢ 9 8 6 3
♣ 9 6 4 3 2

WEST
♠ 9 5 4 3
♡ 9 6
♢ A Q J 4
♣ A 8 7

EAST
♠ K J 8
♡ 8 5
♢ K 10 7 5 2
♣ K 10 5

SOUTH
♠ A 10 6
♡ A K Q J 10 7 4 2
♢ —
♣ Q J

Carmen, dealer, vulnerable versus not, dealt herself a 2-count. "*La Pique Dame*, my only high card," she thought before realizing that she was drifting into Tchaikovsky's eponymous opera instead of Bizet's, where she belonged. "Spades represent death," as she sings in her Card Aria. "And this, a hand with 2 HCP—the cards never lie."

She passed, and Salome gazed at a more-or-less average hand, but she was no average gal. The unpleasantness with John The Baptist had affected her in a peculiar way: Because the left profile of the jack of spades bore an unsettling resemblance to the disciple's severed head as she paraded him on a silver platter, she had fallen victim to a psychological block. She tended to conceal that freighted card, and so she did here as she passed.

Tosca was not passing. She opened one heart, hearts being this ardent lady's favorite suit. To her left, arch-enemy Scarpia snarled a double. He carried a lot of resentment toward Tosca, who, ironically, had been the agent of his demise just when he thought he had her in the palm of his evil hand.

"Pass," intoned Carmen, fearing the worst. Cards unerringly proclaimed one's fate—that was common knowledge among her new friends, the gypsies. "Three diamonds," said Salome. Tosca pondered; her hand was worth four hearts, but, desperate to ensnare Scarpia and to repay him for his treachery towards her lover, Cavarodossi, she chose three hearts, a tactical underbid.

"Four diamonds," growled Scarpia. He lacked the values, but as he was the Chief of Police, he was never doubled if his opponents valued life or family. This was passed around to Tosca, who competed with four hearts, delighted that her plan had matured. Scarpia passed, a shadow of doubt crossing his suspicious mind; Carmen muttered a stoic pass; and Salome doubled—her side had plenty of HCP, and Tosca's bidding wasn't confident. Table presence was never Salome's strong suit, else she would have sensed that her lewd behavior wouldn't play well, even to the debauched court of her stepfather, King Herod. Everyone passed.

Scarpia led a low spade. He rarely led partner's suit, especially when partner was a woman. Tosca played low from dummy, and Salome, still unaware that she held the spade jack, played the king. Tosca won and contentedly counted 10 tricks, but she dearly wanted to rub the result in Scarpia's flushed face. She drew trumps and advanced the club queen. Scarpia hitched before ducking; it couldn't hurt to send his partner some unauthorized information. Salome won with the king and returned a diamond, ruffed. Tosca now ran all but one of her trumps, Being Italian and therefore possessed of excellent bridge genes, she imagined this to be the ending, based on the evidence of trick one (when East followed with the spade king):

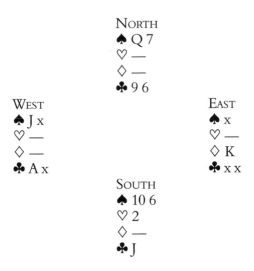

The last trump would strip-squeeze the hated Scarpia and grind garlic salt into his wounded vanity to the tune of a doubled overtrick. However, the actual ending was:

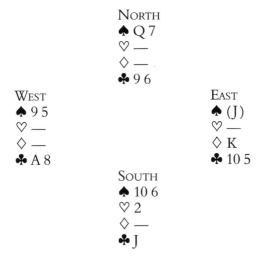

Before making her next play, Tosca leaned across to Carmen and asked: "My dear, is it all right if I risk a laydown, doubled contract to try for a likely overtrick?" Carmen shuddered, as if in the grips of a premonition. *"La carte impitoyable,"* (the card without pity) was all she could muster. Tosca, her French rusty, cashed the last trump.

Scarpia tossed a low spade, giving Tosca pause. Had he blanked the spade jack? Or had he been dealt 5=2=4=2 distribution with the jack-fifth of spades and ace-doubleton of clubs? That would be a stranger takeout double but a more explicable raise to four diamonds. Declarer decided to play for the latter and discarded a club from dummy; Salome, suddenly stricken by the discovery of that unnerving spade jack, didn't follow to the trick at all, but no one noticed, each consumed with individual thoughts—they aren't called divas for nothing.

Tosca exited triumphantly with the club jack. Scarpia won and played a club to Salome's ten. East cashed the diamond king for the setting trick, amid shouts of triumph, shock, and lamentation. Despite the hubbub, Carmen, always a stickler for honesty, no matter the personal cost, noticed that Scarpia was trying to grab the spade jack from Salome's fist and destroy it, before an appeal could be lodged with Valhalla. Tosca was hurrying to throw herself from the nearest parapet.

THE FUTURE AND AN EPILOGUE

The uncertain future of tournament bridge worries anyone who has enjoyed its great benefits. The average age of the ACBL population is nearing seventy. Even accounting for today's longer life spans, that is a troubling figure. Young people have an image of bridge as a senior-citizen activity, and today's youths have many alternate forms of entertainment, especially with the rising popularity of social media. Bridge no longer enjoys the prominence it once had.

To attract youth has been a recruiting mantra for the ACBL. Tournaments restricted to young people are being promoted, not only in America but worldwide, emphasizing the camaraderie as much as the competition. The ACBL-sponsored Collegiate Championships are another encouraging sign. It is also necessary to embrace the computer age and the Internet, mother's milk of the younger generations. Steps in that direction have been taken—a person can play bridge online, either for entertainment, practice, or for masterpoints. Because it is so easy to cheat online (simply have a second computer to literally wire boards to your partner or confederates), the masterpoint awards are reduced from the traditional format. It represents a dilution of masterpoint value, but that may be a necessary price to pay to interest the young. If new young players can sit at their terminals and not worry about appearance or even manners, they may get hooked on the intellectual stimulus and competition that bridge provides. Socialization can come later, as it generally does.

At the high end of the spectrum, the elite players need new stimuli. After winning dozens (or hundreds) of titles and zillions of masterpoints, what is left to accomplish? The answer is money—tournaments with substantial cash awards. To establish even a mini tour, such as golf and tennis enjoy, involves serious challenges. Hefty entry fees will discourage all but the top experts from entering. Sponsorship must be sought, and this is not an easy sell, particularly in the United States. In Europe, for instance, a few cash tournaments have been held in resorts, with tobacco and alcohol sponsors donating a large portion of the prize pool. The hotels also kick in, glad to attract customers in slack seasons. Attempts to attract similar sponsorship in America so far have been unsuccessful. Perhaps computer-related businesses might be tempted.

One obstacle to widespread exposure of bridge is the complexity of the game, especially as played at the top levels. The average player who might enjoy kibitzing such tournaments online, a capability already in place, is likely to be turned off by the proliferation of numerous conventions and non-standard defensive carding agreements. The average golfer or tennis player can comprehend the game he is witnessing, albeit at a fantastically higher level. The bridge spectator is apt to throw up his hands in bewilderment and switch channels if he can't understand even the opening bid and response, or the opening lead.

One fairly obvious solution is to require the competitors to play a simple, standardized system. Disallow complexities to present the game in an easily digested form. The greater the exposure of money bridge to spectators and press, the easier to attract sponsorship. Of course, if the median age of a tournament player is a senior citizen, the products that are advertised necessarily aim at an older, less-lucrative market. Bridge desperately needs youth. Recently, young teams have made their mark in the premier knockout events. They make good "poster children" for the game (most are in their early thirties), but there aren't enough of them.

The ACBL has resisted cash tournaments, in large part because cash substitutes a different incentive from the reliable carrot of masterpoints. The other objection, frequently voiced, is that players will be tempted to cheat when money is at stake, but there have been several notable cheating incidents (review Chapter 7) when the only prize was pride. In fact, the Cavendish Calcutta, America's long-established big-money invitational tournament, has been notably free from innuendo and accusations. People usually cheat for psychological reasons that have little or nothing to do with money.

However, the threat of cheating in our electronic age is a fact of life. Even chess, a game where cheating seemed impossible to conceive, has been besmirched. At least one chess grandmaster is alleged to have relied on outside analytical help during tournaments, relayed to him electronically, perhaps during bathroom breaks. Bridge committees, charged with keeping the game clean, are well aware of the dangers inherent in small, easily-concealed devices that can transmit information, such as "Bid a slam on Board 17," or "East holds a club void on Board 23." There's no fail-safe practical method to stop cheats; recall that a few international players tried to cheat even behind screens. The ugly side of human nature will have its sway, but no scandal has ever derailed bridge.

Perhaps the day will arrive when the women's events are no longer a separate entity. Women have sought and achieved equality in so many areas, why not bridge? There doesn't seem to be any biological reason for the men to play better. As of this writing, recent research debunks the myth that people are dominated by either the left or right hemispheres of their brain, the left being associated with analysis, logic, and math skills, while the right features creativity and emotional sensitivity. Scientists claim that most people use both sides of their brains in tandem—lateralization of function is the norm, and there is no gender bias. For myself, a life involved with high-level bridge and music certainly implies full use of both hemispheres.

If all this is so, it follows that women and men should be equally endowed to play expert-level bridge, and championship-caliber women are demonstrably willing and able to dedicate the necessary prodigious amounts of time and effort to the game. Maybe the tipping point will come when a few women regularly begin to finish at or near the top in open, blue-ribbon events. Perhaps then, other leading women will form teams and compete successfully in open events, liberating themselves from the self-limiting nature of women's events.

Every strong, aspiring player has always known that the best way to improve is to play with and against the best competition you can find. It will be a grand day indeed when the female trailblazers eradicate the stigma of women being regarded as second-tier bridge experts.

*　　　*　　　*

I wrote the following on May 18, 2002, at the invitation of Mark B. W. Lombard who solicited submissions from bridge notables. The Bridge Club of Center City in Philadelphia created a Wall of Fame, covered with inspirational messages to inspire other players. It seems a fitting way to conclude this book.

GRANDER THAN A GOOD CARD PLAYER

"Bridge is valid at either a social or competitive level, and that is part of its charm. For the aspiring tournament player, success at competitive bridge requires substantial strength combined with a delicate sensitivity—indeed, among the best components of human potential. Strength is needed in terms of mental toughness to withstand the inevitable adverse results. Strength also means the ability to play at one's personal peak, even if fatigued or distracted. Strength can amount to physical stamina and conditioning to handle the strain of multiple-session events.

And then there is strength of character that must embrace sportsmanship to the opponents and sensitivity to partner. Your all-important partner deserves heightened sensitivity. Not just sensitivity to the technical messages partner transmits during the auction or defense, although that is important. Just as important is cultivating an awareness of partner's state of mind. Be supportive when all is not going well, because your chance of success surely depends upon partner's performance.

In the end, simultaneously strive to create an imposing aura where the opponents are hard-pressed to produce their best, all the while promoting a calm atmosphere that encourages partner to shine. Hope to become a feared, yet respected, opponent while being a sympathetic and coveted partner. Then, you will have achieved something much grander than being a good card player."

ABOUT THE AUTHOR

Augie Boehm has been a columnist for the American Contract Bridge League's *Bridge Bulletin* and a staff writer for *The Bridge World* magazine for about 20 years. He joined the Goren Editorial Board in 1980.

His path to bridge expertise began in 1961 at the first Junior National Championship in Washington D.C. when he won the title at age 14, the youngest competitor. He has won countless tournaments since.

Augie has taught bridge in and around New York City for over four decades. He is the author of many books, and currently conducts bridge seminars worldwide. An accomplished pianist, he performs regularly at Carnegie Hall. His most recent recording is a classical-music album, *It's A Pleasure*.

BOOKS BY AUGIE BOEHM

Big Deal
Boehm's Basic Bridge Book
Boehm's Card Play Essentials
Demon Defense and Demon Doubling
Matchpoints Versus IMPs
Private Sessions: A Bridge Education
Three Notrump in Depth
Wielding The Axe: The Vanishing Art of the Penalty Double

For more information, visit The Bridge World at:
www.bridgeworld.com

ABOUT THE BRIDGE WORLD

Since 1929, *The Bridge World* has been the world's leading authority on the game of bridge, where players learn the secrets of winning from the biggest names in the game.

Every monthly issue of *The Bridge World* is focused on improving readers' understanding of the game and on advancing technique through quizzes and contests on bidding, play and defense; analytical tournament reports; thematic articles; interviews; unbiased book reviews; and puzzles. The renown Master Solvers Club and Challenge the Champs features appear in each issue and enable development of advanced bidding judgment and partnership rapport.

The magazine presents humorous articles alongside cutting-edge theories and method improvements in bidding and defensive-card-play agreements. Virtually every major advance in the history of the game was first presented or developed in the pages of *The Bridge World*. Readers can follow the newest developments in the game as they unfold and keep up with the inner workings of high-level bridge. The magazine provides the inside story of current affairs and objective looks at the decisions of policymakers and legislators.

The Bridge World is an invaluable learning tool for any serious bridge player wishing to reach a higher level.

Visit The Bridge World on the web at:
www.bridgeworld.com
• Sample articles and subscription information
• Other books published by *The Bridge World*
• Online store featuring a wide selection of
bridge books, software, and accessories
• Bridge learning center
• The Master Solvers Club monthly contest
and much more . . .